Cartoons and Lampoons

THE ART OF POLITICAL SATIRE

Cartoons and Lampoons

THE ART OF POLITICAL SATIRE

Samuel A. Tower

JULIAN MESSNER
NEW YORK

All rights reserved including the right of
reproduction in whole or in part in any form.
Published by Julian Messner, a Simon & Schuster
Division of Gulf & Western Corporation,
Simon & Schuster Building,
1230 Avenue of the Americas,
New York, New York 10020.
JULIAN MESSNER and colophon are trademarks of
Simon & Schuster, registered in the U.S. Patent
and Trademark Office.

Manufactured in the United States of America.
Design by Irving Perkins Associates

Library of Congress Cataloging in Publication Data

Tower, Samuel A.
Cartoons and lampoons.

Includes index.
1. United States—Politics and government—
Caricatures and cartoons. 2. American wit and
humor, Pictorial—History. I. Title.
E183.T73   741.5′0973   82-3500
ISBN 0-671-34064-6   AACR2

Cartoons and Lampoons

THE ART OF POLITICAL SATIRE

CHAPTER I

IF a picture is worth a thousand words, as the saying goes, then the cartoon—not the comic cartoon but the cartoon of commentary—is worth a thousand volumes. What is this cartoon with so much impact and influence? It is the editorial cartoon that appears every day in the newspaper. Usually it is on the editorial page in which the newspaper expresses its opinions, though some newspapers put their cartoons on the front page. Editorial cartoons also appear in a number of weekly and monthly magazines. In all cases, the editorial cartoon expresses a point of view: on the conflict between the West and Communism, on coping with the high cost of living, on the spread of pollution, on the dangers of taking drugs, on the "boner" expressed by a public figure.

The cartoon expresses a point of view as a drawing by the pen of a gifted artist rather than words from the pen or typewriter of a writer of editorials. It is a drawing that takes up a vital issue of the day. One concentrated drawing cuts through to the essentials of an issue. For the editorial cartoonist, there is none of the "on the one hand" and "on the other hand" that editorial writers use on the way to formulating their conclusions. With a few strokes of the pen, the cartoonist makes a declaration: this is the issue and this where I stand on it. There is no room for ifs, ands, or buts in an editorial cartoon.

In his autobiography, *Drawn from Memory*, the longtime cartoonist of *The Chicago Tribune*, John McCutcheon wrote: "The cartoon differs from any other picture in that the idea alone is the essential requirement, whether it is meant to inform, reform, or solely to amuse. This idea should be brought out with directness and simplicity, in such a way that people will know it is a cartoon and not a work of art. It has little to do with beauty or grace; it has much to do with strength and uniqueness. It is a peculiar form of art for a peculiar purpose, and presupposes the ability to say things trenchantly, humorously, or caustically, expressed through a drawing."

The idea that a picture is worth so many words is not really selling words short. The three words "I love you" are more expressive than any picture, and one clear paragraph may be worth more than a lot of unclear pictures or complicated charts. What the saying suggests is that one picture of a grieving face may express more than all the mournful elegies since Homer. Human beings' primary contact with the universe is visual, which accounts for cave paintings, religious images, and much of the impulse of boy-meets-girl and marriage. The impact of one image is a thousand times more immediate than the impact of a thousand words. What's more, seeing is automatic, while reading takes training, and there was a time when few people in the world could read or write. In any culture, the drawing, the piece of sculpture, the

"My colleagues and I are convinced we'll find intelligent beings . . ." "Cartoon Countdown" by Bernard Wiseman.

fables of the gods, the spoken words of a play—all came hundreds of years before written literature.

These are all forms of communication. The cartoon, too, is a form of communication, and one of the earliest. Caricature, expressed in cartoons, goes back to the earliest days of civilization. The ancient Egyptians, along with their pyramids and monuments, left behind drawings that caricatured the foibles and weaknesses of their fellows. Even before the Egyptians, a prehistoric cartoonist may have carved an unflattering likeness of an inept hunter or a bossy caveman on the side of a Stone Age cave. In the case of Stone Age people, it may be hard to separate a real likeness from a caricature. But there is no mistaking the savage caricatures found in the wilds of Africa, Siberia, and North America, or the unflattering likeness of his officer that a Roman soldier of A.D. 79 scratched on the wall of his barrack in Pompeii, preserved by the ashes of Vesuvius to this day. In fact, the sport of cartooning fellow human beings seems to occur in many nations, ancient and modern, pagan and Christian. Much as the ancients differed from us, they certainly laughed at one another, just as we do, and for precisely the same reasons—and they employed every art, device, and implement of ridicule that is known to modern man.

In India, the mother of tradition and ancient beliefs, there is sometimes a touch of the burlesque in the images of the gods, especially Krishna, the Don Juan of India's deities, whose images are often less than that of solemn majesty. The figures on ancient temples of Southeast Asia are depicted participating in activities more fun-loving than worshipful, as associated with the Almighty in the West. The Chinese, who, according to tradition, taught the Greeks the secrets of art, often seem to make fun in the paintings of their gods. Egypt's art was already old when Greek art was young, and it remained crude when Greek art reached the heights of greatness. But its crudity did not hinder the Egyptian delight in caricature and cartoon. There is a specimen of the kind of cartoon favored by the Egyptians that dates back more than 3,000 years. It depicts, clearly and strikingly on its slab of limestone, servants carrying their drunken master home from a banquet. Greece and Rome learned from Egypt the practice of caricaturing the actions of humans by picturing animals doing the same thing. The world today is not too far from ancient Egypt when one thinks of the United States with its Republican elephant and Democratic donkey behaving like good Democrats and Republicans. Just as we do today, the Egyptians regarded their rulers as fair game. Cartoons on tombs at Thebes depict the faults of pharaohs, and even Cleopatra, the seductive and beautiful, is portrayed in various stages of intoxication. It may be surprising to find cartoons in a tomb, but the Egyptians recorded every detail of their lives and history on their monuments—so why not a bit of accurate caricature?

The gods and goddesses were the targets of the caricaturists and comedy writers of Greece, though little cartooning remains, except on some pottery. The Romans, in addition to lampooning passing events and social excesses, found a special target for cartooning—the Christians. The walls of every Roman town testified to the cartoonists' delight in contemptuous caricature of those trouble makers, the early Christians. In the Middle Ages,

Ancient Egyptian cartoons lampooning drinking habits.

with Christianity triumphant, caricature found its greatest expression, in, of all places, the carvings and decorations of the cathedrals. Some of the most naughty were obliterated by the priests themselves. Not only on stone but in the sacred books used in the churches there are brilliantly illuminated pictures done in a most irreverent style. Cartoonists were busy during the Reformation. Martin Luther himself was no mean cartoonist, ridiculing the Pope, the cardinals, and the bishops through pictures. When Luther got married, there was a flood of cartoons from his enemies. Even the Puritans in England in the early 1600's used caricature to attempt to persuade the Protestants in the Netherlands to join them.

Out of this background of centuries of graphic art in a light, poking-fun vein, in the 1600's drawings as specific weapons of ridicule emerged. Some two centuries were to pass before the political cartoon achieved its mature form and definitive function. Anyone who reads the ancient journals knows that while nothing may seem as old as yesterday's news, nothing seems fresher than the old political cartoons. To satirize events and the makers of events, the cartoon refines material until only the essential satiric essence remains. Circumstances impossible in the real world are portrayed on the cartoonists' stage— the politician comes face to face with his broken prom-

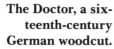

The Doctor, a six-teenth-century German woodcut.

ises, hypocrisy assumes a human face, fingers are pointed, blame is fixed, and responsibility gets pinned on figures with recognizable faces. There are liabilities in this. The cartoon's first obligation is to be pithy; faces and facts may be stretched to make a point. There is a lack of shading and subtlety. Political cartoonists work best "against" rather than "for" something. As Adolph Ochs, the founder of the *New York Times* once noted: "A cartoon cannot say 'On the other hand. . .' " But a cartoon can often do what words cannot. By overstating, by heating up an issue, it can bring action—and it has. In addition, the cartoon provides a graphic perspective on its times, a kind of time capsule of history in sixteen square inches of paper. One of the brightest American cartoonists of the 1980's is Jeff MacNelly of the *Richmond News Leader* of Virginia, who is just in his thirties. "Political cartoonists," says MacNelly, "misquote, trifle with the truth, make science fiction out of politics. But when the smoke clears, the political cartoonist has been getting closer to the truth than the guys who write political opinions." Today—and for many yesterdays—the great cartoon has been very close to the truth, worth a thousand words and often many, many more.

CHAPTER II

THE cartoon, like so many things, did not always mean what it means now. In fact, up to about a century or so ago, the word *cartoon* still meant much the same as it did in the days of Leonardo da Vinci and Raphael: a preliminary drawing, executed in full scale and often in color, of the design to be carried out in tapestry, mosaic, mural painting, or other major work of art. It was usually done on a heavy or durable paper and got its name from the Italian *cartone*, a large sheet of paper. When the cartoon was used for tapestry, it was usually placed by the loom so that the weaver could see it clearly just beside his work and use it as a guide. Today, a "cartoon" serving as a guide for a work of art would be called a layout.

The earliest crucibles of caricature (what we now think of as cartoons) were Italy and Holland. In Italy, at the close of the sixteenth century, there was the studio of the brothers Carracci and their followers, who delighted in playing artistic games in drawing their friends. Annibale Carracci gave the name *caricatura* to the comic drawings he made to amuse his friends. The name comes from an Italian verb meaning to load up, as with exaggerated detail. Annibale Carracci even provided the earliest definition of the aims of the cartoonist, a definition that still stands up: "Is not the task of the caricaturist exactly the same as that of the classical artist? Both see the lasting truth behind the surface of mere outward appearance. Both try to help nature accomplish its plan. The one may strive to visualize the perfect form and to realize it in his work, the other to grasp the perfect deformity, and thus reveal the very essence of a personality. A good caricature, like every work of art, is more true to life than reality itself."

Two of the early great painters of the Netherlands, Hieronymous Bosch and Pieter Brueghel the Elder, display a sense of caricature. Bosch's hellish, exaggerated creatures are scary, but Brueghel's works show the true spirit of caricature: his Rabelaisian paintings show Flemish peasants guzzling, stuffing themselves, lusting, dancing, harvesting—all larger than life on his crowded canvases. Some art historians believe da Vinci and Dürer were early exponents of portrait caricature, but their grotesque sketches are more likely experimental drawings rather than actual caricature. Some historians also find the spirit of caricature in the gargoyles on the gothic churches and the goblins on the margins of medieval manuscripts. No one can say for sure, but more likely the goblins and gargoyles served as reminders of the creatures of hell. During the Reformation period, all kinds of crude woodcuts appeared holding up various people to ridicule. Closer to caricature were the studies of drunks, gamblers, and lechers by a group of Dutch artists of the early years of the seventeenth century. From Italy, caricature spread to the rest of Europe, especially to France and England, and became the rage.

"Young man," said the Duchess of Marlborough in a letter to a friend in 1710, "you come from Italy. They tell me of a new invention there called Caricatura drawing. Can you tell me someone that will draw me a caricature of Lady Masham, describing her covered with running sores and ulcers, that I might send to the Queen?"

With the emergence in 1720 of the gifted English pictorial satirist, painter, and engraver, William Hogarth, the cartoon came of age, not long after the Duchess of Marlborough uttered these words. He is considered by many to be the father of cartooning, and none of his many descendants has been his equal. Hogarth did not even have to search for a vision of the world to portray in his cartooning. He was born within view of London's Newgate Prison, filled with debtors and highway robbers, with markets, fairgrounds, and a hospital nearby, surrounded by life. In his early thirties he became famous overnight with a series of sketches about the life of a prostitute. Then came a series about a licentious man-about-town driven mad by his overindulgence. Further series on marriage, medicine, politics, and other facets of English life followed. All his compositions are crowded, but every detail is in place. Along with his painting he kept on producing prints to show how art should serve society. Hogarth rarely depicted personalities in his satire, nor did he, as a rule, take any particular event as a subject; he looked much more widely over the whole range of human frailties, selecting and staging them as

17

An engraving made in 1750 by William Hogarth entitled, "Gin Lane."

a stage manager. Hogarth was appalled by both the moral corruption that was rife throughout eighteenth century high society and the awful conditions of those in the London slums, and his prints focus on both evils. The people he indicted shouted their pleasure at his droll art and bought his prints. Not that all of Hogarth's prints made a moralistic point. A goodly number of scenes of English life, rich in sharply observed and deftly executed detail, were done solely for pleasure. But his style and his best work owe much to the devices of caricature. The key issues, the gravest problems of his day, were the content of his prints. In his series on elections, for example, he depicts the public swindled of their votes by politicians, their right to an elected government being stolen by the party bosses and the hucksters of the time. His cartoons focused on social issues such as bribery, cruelty, prison abuses, the liquor business, and child labor. His cartoons are now classics and his influence on the development of cartooning was profound and indelible. What was little more than a sophisticated fad when Hogarth began to use his pen matured, in his hands, into some of the greatest graphic art of the West.

During the Hogarth period, cartoons were not printed in newspapers, as they are today, but as posters or handbills, sometimes even on objects like ladies' fans. The print shops and print sellers put out collections of the cartoons, which were rented for the evening by people who were giving parties and wished to entertain their guests with a fashionable amusement.

If William Hogarth represented the artist as moralist, one of his most distinguished successors, Thomas Rowlandson, was the artist as the easy-going, sophisticated gay blade. His sardonic pen delineated laughing indignation but never just moralizing. During Rowlandson's lifetime, George III became king of England and fumbled away the American colonies, the French Revolution took place, and Napoleon rose and fell. Rowlandson the cartoonist had things to say about the men and women who were actors in these events. Artists got no royalties in those days—a printer's plate was sold outright—so Rowlandson was always hunting for new subject matter. He drew the dancing bears, the fancy balls, the fat old men slugging away their wine, the masked ladies going to meet their lovers, the three-bottle parson, the foibles and woes of English life. His engravings were quickly done, quickly printed and colored, and swiftly snapped up. They were not the careful work of Hogarth, nor is the detail laid on. Rowlandson's work has the grace of an artist who puts in only what is needed. His people rush to play or parade, strut, or make love with the pleasure of well-drawn bodies aware that time on earth is short.

In 1812 Rowlandson introduced the first regular cartoon character when he brought out the first series of illustrated escapades featuring a bony, lantern-jawed, pedantic old parson called Doctor Syntax. The highly successful *Tour of Dr. Syntax in Search of the Picturesque* was followed in 1820 by *Dr. Syntax in Search of Consolation* and in 1821 by *Dr. Syntax in Search of a Wife.* The three volumes make up a grand tour of English society, a picture of an age and a people. Although "speech balloons" and horizontal banks of framed pictures had been used in prints before he did so, Rowlandson was the first to make use continuously and systematically of these stock con-

A caricature entitled, "The Successful Fortune Hunter." It was engraved by Thomas Rowlandson in 1802.

ventions of the cartoon strip, so familiar to readers of today's newspapers.

Even more of an influence in the development of the political cartoon than Hogarth and Rowlandson was James Gillray, another great successor of Hogarth. Without Gillray, who was the leading English cartoonist when that bumbling monarch, George III, was on the throne, modern cartoonists might have been without method or symbols. Gillray invented many of the stock figures of international events and incidents still in use. The English, German, French, and Russian characters symbolizing those nations that he invented are still in common use in modern times. Gillray was also a magnificent engraver, working directly on the copper plate without previous drawings, and, alone of his generation's famous artists, included experiments with the new art of lithography among his huge output.

Much of this output, coarse by any standards, was directed against George III, whom Gillray bitterly opposed and whom he delighted in portraying as "Farmer George." He mocked the unroyal stinginess of King George and Queen Charlotte. Sickened by the French Revolution, he put out a deluge of cartoons savagely attacking its bloody excesses and then turned his fire on Napoleon, greatly enraging his subject. But the sharpness of his pen was by no means reserved only for the French. With equal venom he aimed his graphic darts at the leading British political figures of his day and on ideas he regarded with contempt and amusement. Gillray was vicious, coarse, and unrestrained, but in his choice of targets he approached the modern-day cartoonist.

After Gillray, fire-and-brimstone cartooning dimin-

DUMOURIER dining in State at S.t James's, on the 15.th of May 1793. Vide The own Declaration printed by the Anti-levelling Soc.y

To the worthy Members of the Society at the CROWN & ANCHOR, this Print illustrative of Treasons in Embryo (by them hunted out & exposed) is submitted by an admirer of their Loyal principles & truly Classic publications

James Gillray drew this satirical cartoon in 1793. The head of King George III is on a platter.

ished, and a more genteel approach to political cartoons emerged with George Cruikshank, the son of Isaac Cruikshank, himself a distinguished political cartoonist. George Cruikshank did, however, manifest Gillray's artistic gusto as he spread his great talent over much of the nineteenth century. He lived to be nearly ninety and worked in the entire field of illustration (he was a noted book illustrator) without once drawing a picture that for

23

any reason he would wish to turn to the wall. Cruikshank was a warrior who fought with his pen against the evils of drink, which he attacked in an extended series of cartoons. He turned out vast numbers of drawings lampooning the political figures of his day, collections of which were published under the title, "The Political House That Jack Built." Cruikshank produced them with the pamphleteer, William Hone; such pamphlets were the first to join the talents of the political cartoonist to words upholding partisan views. Before their appearance, cartoons could be acquired only as single sheet illustrations or in serial groupings that were on display and sold in the London print shops. The pamphlets were the forerunners of the present-day satirical magazines containing cartoons.

To continue the roll of pioneering giants of political cartooning, one must cross the English Channel to France. The early 1800's were a time when the old world of glory was disappearing and the modern world was being born. Honoré Daumier depicted this world in almost 4,000 lithographs, many done for the political publications of his lifelong friend, Charles Philipon. The publications raised caricature from a print seller's venture to a valid form of journalism that poked fun at a society seeking gold and pleasure and aimed even sharper barbs at the mighty in government. Some credit Daumier with being the originator of the modern cartoon because of his uncrowded sketches, his powerful character portrayal, his use of black and white, and the impact of his work, overwhelmingly moving in its simplicity. Daumier spent six months in prison for the way he portrayed the disliked King Louis Philippe, who was placed on the throne after

An 1834 lithograph by Daumier entitled, "The Legislative Body."

Napoleon's fall. The king didn't like being pictured as a bulbous pear (made worse because the French word for pear carries the slang meaning, "fathead"), or Daumier's depicting him as Rabelais's ugly giant, Gargantua. Daumier exposed the wrongs of his time with ridicule and heightened viewers' perception of these injustices with an absurd simplicity (or so it appeared). But he also managed to communicate sympathy and understanding, no matter how sharp his cartoons. Daumier broke down the barriers that had separated "serious" art from the art of caricature and made it possible for the "serious" artist to experiment with facial expression and distortion. He paved a way for the Expressionism of twentieth century art.

Gustave Doré, somewhat younger than Daumier, was famous for his humorous, extravagant wood-engraved book illustrations. Many of Doré's techniques, such as the use of "zoom" lines to suggest speed and rapid jumps from distant to close-up views, foreshadowed stock devices of the modern comic strip.

As the nineteenth century approached its midpoint, newspapers, satirical weekly magazines, and technical changes brought the political cartoon into a new era—the era of the modern cartoonist, who, with a few strokes of the pen, comments on the momentous events of an ever changing world.

CHAPTER III

IN 1754, in the American colonies, a cartoon appeared in the *Pennsylvania Gazette,* the newspaper published by Benjamin Franklin. It was a crude woodcut depicting a snake divided into segments, each one bearing the initials of one of Britain's American colonies from New England to Georgia. Below the severed serpent was the caption: "Unite or die." The cartoon was prompted by the outbreak of the French and Indian War. The war put the colonies in such danger, in Franklin's view, that the only way they could overcome was to stand united— or fall.

Eleven years later, in 1765, the British Parliament undertook a series of measures and taxes that the colonists viewed as infringements on their rights. The principal of these was the Stamp Act, levied directly on consumers for such items as playing cards and marriage licenses. It was a trifling tax, but if accepted it might have become a wedge for heavier taxes. Franklin believed that this peril, too, could be overcome by united effort. The author of *Poor Richard's Almanack* and of such maxims as "A penny

Ben Franklin's famous "Unite or Die" snake cartoon.

saved is a penny earned" showed his characteristic thrift. He dusted off the old divided snake cartoon and reprinted it, to even greater effect. Ultimately, delegates from nine colonies met in 1765, in what they called the Stamp Act Congress, to oppose the measure. And eventually, Britain repealed the Stamp Act. It would be nice to credit this to the power of Franklin's cartoon. In truth, far more potent was a boycott of British goods, accompanied by the application of a coat of tar and feathers to boycott violators. The point made by the cartoon stood up, however: the boycott united the American people for the first time in common action.

An interesting fact is that Franklin had a moving encounter with Hogarth, without question the father of English cartoonists. Franklin, whose many talents in-

"The Bostonians Paying the Excise Man," a 1774 cartoon printed in London.

cluded diplomacy, was living in London before the Revolution as a representative of Pennsylvania, and he became intimately acquainted with Hogarth. The very last letter the dying Hogarth received was from Dr. Franklin; his answer was dictated only three hours before his death.

Whether Franklin should get credit for fathering the American cartoon is debatable. Franklin's illustration was indeed a political cartoon and was published in an American newspaper; but it had no immediate consequence for the art of cartooning—it did not establish cartooning as an element of journalism. Nearly a hundred years were to pass before that came about.

This is not to say that the period before the Revolution was totally devoid of cartoons. In addition to his famous severed snake, Franklin distributed in England a poignant cartoon in 1774, two years before the Declaration of Independence. In 1774, he believed the colonies' best interests were bound up with those of England, and he tried in every way to arouse English public feeling against policies that would spur a complete break. The cartoon depicts Britannia sliding off the world—her limbs severed, her ships without sail, the English oaks withered as it prophesies the sad plight of Britannia stripped of her colonies.

Ironically, Franklin, who was the first to publish cartoons in America, appears to be the first man to be ridiculed in one. He became the target of a series of crude cartoons accusing him of double-dealing as a result of his entanglement in the conflict between the Quakers, who were friendly to the Indians, and the Scotch, Irish, and German elements, who were anti-Quaker and anti-Indian.

For the most part, political satire in the American colonies took literary form. Lampoons, parodies, and satirical ballads were published in almanacs, pamphlets, and, after 1704, in newspapers. There were numerous writers and printers but few skilled at drawing or engraving. Some crude woodcuts were produced on single printed sheets. Those reporting the "last words" of executed criminals, often embellished by a rough woodcut depicting an actual hanging, were highly popular.

The beginnings of a native school of American graphic satire can perhaps be traced back to the work of Paul Revere, silversmith, engraver, and staunch rebel, who had begun his publishing career by distributing copies of English prints sympathetic to the American cause. The few painters and engravers living and working in America before the Revolution were active, like Paul Revere, in silversmithing, pottery, sign-painting, and other skilled crafts. Opportunities for engraving were neither numerous nor lucrative.

The Americans had early and continuous supporters in England, who expressed themselves in words and in numerous cartoons as favorable to the colonies and against King George III. British support was spearheaded by Whigs like William Pitt, Charles James Fox, and Edmund Burke, who identified the colonists' struggle with their own fight against an autocratic king. The king's woes were aggravated by his going from one minister to another as he cast about for a man of ability; he finally settled on Lord North, who proved to be a disaster. In Britain, the king was caricatured as a despot, or a skinflint, or as "Farmer George." Another cartoon shows North, Fox, and Burke as strange bedfellows doing a

dance around a wooden bust of "King Wisdom III." A
1775 cartoon demonstrated that to many Britons war in
America spelled doom: it depicts King George, eyes shut,
drawn by horses of obstinacy and pride into a chasm, as
America burns and the Magna Carta is trampled. Another British cartoon makes the point more simply: it
shows the horse "America" throwing its master. A 1776
Whig cartoon shows Tory ministers, swords drawn, about
to kill the goose that lays the golden eggs, symbolizing
the American colonies.

The Americans used a few British cartoons as sources
for their own cartoons depicting their problems with
England. Among the first such source was one called
"The Deplorable State of America." The English cartoon is much better drawn, has fewer figures and fewer
symbols, and makes its point more clearly and with much
less fuss. The American engraver, Wilkinson, wanted his
audience not only to get the point, but not to miss any of
the points, and so he produced an elaborate plate,
abounding with symbols and loops containing comments. To top it all off, he felt obliged to furnish an
explanation that was printed in the *Pennsylvania Gazette*
of November 21, 1765. The seriousness of the situation
comes through, despite the passage of more than two
centuries, and the picture is augmented by the contemporary flavor of the language. It reads:

On the Fatal First of November, 1765, was published a caricature Print representing the deplorable state of America, and
under what Influence her ruin is Attempted. At the Top is a
Figure representing France holding in one hand a Purse of
Money to a Comet, marked with a Jack-Boot, and out of her
mouth a Label by which we find she actuates the Star to shed

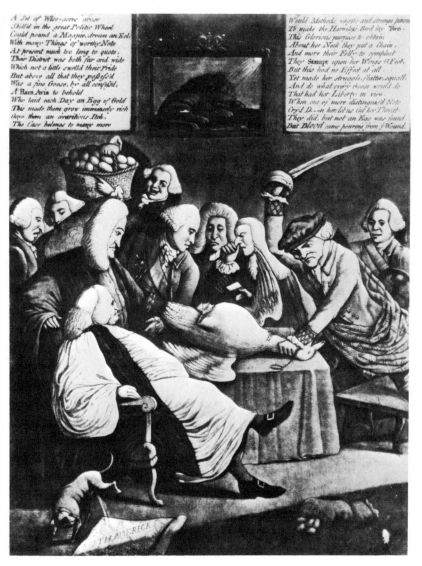

Britain killing the goose of the American colonies, as drawn by an English cartoonist.

its baneful Influence on Britannia; who presents a box to America, telling her it is the Stamp Act; but on it is wrote: Pandora's Box (which according to the Poets was filled with all kinds of Calamities). America, who is in deep distress, calls out to Minerva to secure her, for she abhors it as death! Minerva (i.e., Wisdom) forbids her taking it, and points to Liberty who is expiring at the feet of America with a label proper to his extremity. Close by is a fair Tree inscribed to Liberty; at whose roots grows a Thistle, from under it creeps a viper, and infixes its sting in the side of Liberty. Mercury (who signifies Commerce) reluctantly leaves America, as is expressed by the Label. Boreas near the Comet, blows a violent Gust full upon the Tree of Liberty; against which Loyalty leans and expresses her fear of losing her support. Behind, a Number of Ships, hauled up, and to be sold; a Crowd of Sailors, dismissed, with Labels proper to them. On the other side, a Gallows, with this Inscription: Fit Entertainment for Stamp Men. A Number of these Gentlemen, with labels expressing various Sentiments on the Occasion. At the Bottom is a Coat of Arms, proper for the Stamp Men.

All that in one cartoon!

George Washington figures in only a few cartoons; this is not because everyone thought he was a superb commander-in-chief or because he was so beloved that there was not a dissenting vote when he was chosen to be the first President. It is probable that cartoons critical of Washington were destroyed in the patriotic fervor of the victorious new nation. A 1777 British cartoon shows the American leaders as animals chased out of the "Cave of Rebellion" by the British lion, with John Hancock as a boar, John Adams as a fox, and Washington as an armadillo. In 1783 another British cartoon shows Washington as a woman using a thirteen-tailed whip over the shoulders of a weeping Britannia. A cartoon that appeared in the early days of the Republic, titled "The Entry," was full of disloyal and profane allusions: President Washington is represented as riding on an ass, evoking an association with Christ's entry into Jerusalem; Washington is led by Colonel David Humphreys, the President's aide and secretary, who is singing verses. One of the verses ran: "A glorious time has come to pass when David shall conduct an ass."

More characteristic of his countrymen's feelings for Washington is the cartoon on the cover of *Bickerstaff's Boston Almanack or Federal Calendar for 1788*, the only one known showing Washington and Franklin together. While the cartoon is not well done, the verbal fireworks of the explanatory note more than make up for this. In those days, when the memory of the struggle for hard-won freedom was still fresh, patriotism was unabashed. The note explaining the cartoon was pure red, white, and blue:

The frontispiece represents the truly patriotick Washington and Franklin triumphantly seated in the Federal Chariot drawn by 13 Freemen, figurative of the happy Union now forming by these States. The heroick Washington holds in his hand the grand Fabrick of American Independence, the Federal Constitution, offering it with paternal affection to his freeborn brethren the Sons of Columbia. That staunch Friend and Guardian of the civil and religious Rights of Mankind, the sagacious and philosophick Franklin, sits attentive with spectacles on, having just scan'd over the Glorious Work, which will prove the political Salvation of his Country, holding a Staff, on which is affixed a Cap, allusive of American Freedom, if the Constitution is adopted. The Goddess of Fame, flying with a Trumpet in her hand, spreading the glad Tidings of Union through the States, sounds a peal to the immortal honour of that worthy and disinterested Band of Patriots and Heroes, the 39 members of the late Federal Convention, who, with such Wisdom, sound Judgement, and unbiased Patriotism, framed the present Constitution; whose Names, we trust will be handed down to ages yet unborn, with the highest Veneration and Respect, by every Friend to his Country, for their unshaken Zeal in the Cause of American Freedom.— The Sun, entirely clear of the Horizon, shines resplendently on the American Federal Union, denoting that every ray of light has now burst forth, and beautifully illumines the whole United Continent of America.

The struggle over ratification of the Constitution, bitterly fought among the states, touched off a number of cartoons, as did the later removal of the national capital from New York to Philadelphia. Two-thirds of the thirteen states had to ratify the Constitution, and a triumphant cartoon in the *Massachusetts Centinel* in 1788 hails the "erection of the pillars of the great national dome"; North Carolina and Rhode Island, which had not yet ratified, were depicted as pillars in sorry condition.

A British cartoon of 1782, "The Reconciliation Between Britannia and Her Daughter America," encouraged the progress of the peace talks. Britannia is saying, "Be a good girl and give me a buss." America, depicted as an Indian maiden carrying a liberty bonnet on a spear, is saying, "Dear Mama, say no more about it." Uncle Sam had not yet been invented, and cartoonists commonly depicted the United States as an Indian, an eagle, a rattlesnake, or a bucking horse.

Chapter IV

A cartoon that appeared in the early 1800's has become another American classic, along with Benjamin Franklin's severed snake, with its economy of line and concept. This was the clever creation in 1812 of a new political animal by Elkanah Tisdale, called a "Gerrymander," that made its debut in the *Weekly Messenger* of Boston. (Incidentally, Tisdale, like Franklin, was not a professional cartoonist; he was an engraver.) As politicians are still doing today, the Republican legislature of Massachusetts in 1812 carved the state into new voting districts. In one county, they strung twelve towns together so that the heavy Republican vote of one of them would overbalance the votes of the Federalists in the other eleven towns. On the map the area looked like a lizardlike creature called a salamander. Tisdale added claws, wings, and fangs to the map, and called it a "Gerry-Mander" after the Republican governor Elbridge Gerry. The cartoon helped defeat the governor for reelection though he was elected vice-president with President James Madison the same year. The new districting served the

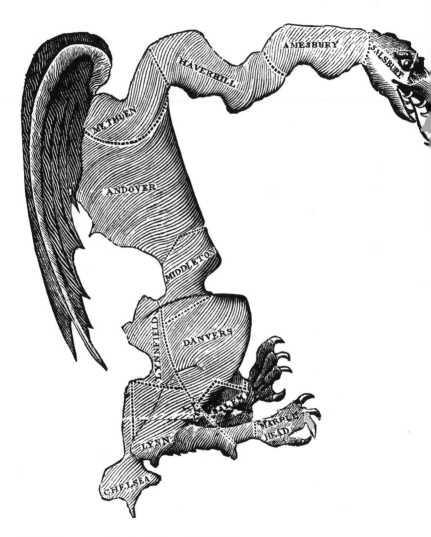

The Gerrymander by Elkanah Tisdale.

Republicans well in the election but so angered the voters that it was repealed the next year. The cartoon introduced a new word, *to gerrymander,* into the language and into American politics.

Washington's death in 1799 perhaps saved him from the humiliation of losing a political fight over the reelection of President John Adams. Nothing could stop the triumphant surge of the Republicans and their candidate, Jefferson. In fact, during Washington's second term, Republican papers had sniped at him continually about his kingly habits. John Adams, the second President, was fat and fussy and fought with every prominent American of his time. He fought especially with other leaders of his Federalist party and gave the leader of the opposing party, Thomas Jefferson, an opportunity to become the next President. The Republicans called Adams a madman and described the Federalists as monarchists, English lovers, warmongers, and spendthrifts and accused them of selling out the country to the moneylenders. The Federalists called the Republicans radical scum and charged that they were seeking to set up an American military dictator like Napoleon. The Republicans swept into power in 1800 and ran the government for forty years.

Cartoons of the early 1800's reflected the same kind of "high-level, gentlemanly" exchanges. They were not good, but they were plentiful. The press at the time had no independent life: newspapers were the servants and slaves of political parties and reflected only partisan viewpoints. Both parties saw to it that their enemies were portrayed as vermin, skunks, foxes, snakes, and porcu-

39

pines in print and cartoons, in the pages of the newspapers they controlled.

The early American cartoons, much different from today's, developed naturally from the techniques of contemporary British cartoonists. In general they were overdrawn, crowded with figures, and brutally satiric. The dialogue "balloons" were squeezed in wherever possible, and the dialogue was both long and illegible. Most newspapers appeared every two weeks, so the cartoonists had plenty of time to make elaborate designs; subtlety, however, was not a strong point. Most artists were anonymous, similar to the unpublicized staff artists who do much modern newspaper illustration. Partisan politics, with no fear of libel laws and no respect for individual dignity, provided the cartoonists with their themes. The issues were whether or not to go to war with England; high tariffs or low tariffs; national banks or local banks; free states or slave states. A few years into the 1800's, events aroused intense feelings that found popular expression in cartoons. Cartooning got more attention both from designers and engravers, and cartoons began to appear with greater frequency. The artists themselves became bolder and they signed their work more often.

The events that enflamed the passions of Americans were the Embargo Act of 1807 and the War of 1812. The Embargo Act was Jefferson's way of taking action against the warring nations, Britain and France, both of which seized American ships and American seamen on the high seas. Since Europe depended so much on U.S. raw materials, Jefferson, rather than go to war, cut off American exports to Europe. The embargo angered Americans from all parts of the nation, while the Europeans managed to get along on smuggled goods. The Embargo Act was repealed in 1809. Three years later, with James Madison as President and the nation facing the same abuses on the oceans, the United States entered armed conflict with Britain in the War of 1812, a war some call the second War of Independence.

"Mad Tom in a Rage" is the title of a Federalist cartoon that attacks Jefferson and makes its point with a minimum of balloons and characters. Jefferson, aided by the Devil and brandy, is trying to pull down the U.S. government structure built by Washington and Adams. The Federalists liked to picture Jefferson as a brandy-soaked anarchist tearing down the edifice of government. The Ograbme, also called the Snapping Terrapin, became another favorite fantasy creature of cartoons. "Ograbme" is the word *embargo* spelled backward. Irate citizens cynically turned *embargo* into "O grab me," "Go bar 'em," "Mob rage" and the "Dembargo." The Federalists, who did most of the illegal smuggling, made the turtle or terrapin a symbol of government oppression. Among the simpler cartoons, one shows a turtle snapping the thigh of a man who is trying to smuggle a barrel of tobacco onto a British ship while the man exclaims, "This cursed Ograbme." There were many others. A cartoonist who signed his work "Peter Pencil" attacked Jefferson with both effectiveness and artistic skill. One of his cartoons shows Jefferson reduced to rags because of the embargo policies, and another shows him being attacked and robbed by both John Bull and Napoleon.

James Madison, who inherited many of Jefferson's woes, was President when a predominantly hawkish Congress forced the declaration of war in 1812. The war provided

INTERCOURSE or Impartial Dealings

An 1809 "Peter Pencil" cartoon showing Jefferson being victimized by England and France.

a cause—freedom of the seas—as well as a chance to wipe out a renewed Indian menace and to try to annex Canada.

American cartoon pioneers of significance emerged during the War of 1812: William Charles, James Akin, Amos Doolittle, Alexander Anderson, and Elkanah Tisdale, already mentioned for his fabulous creature, the gerrymander. The most famous of the early cartoonists was William Charles, a Scot who was forced to leave home because he used his pen too boldly against the clergy and came to the States. His work is much in the style of the British cartoonists Rowlandson and Gillray. In fact, the basis of all these early cartoonists' work was the Gillray grouping of a lot of figures. Extensive dialogue in the balloons and a liberal use of allegory and symbolism, which tended to be stilted and pompous, was also typical. Humor tended to be conspicuous by its absence; what humor there was consisted of an obvious pun. William Charles stands out from the others because his cartoons purveyed a rough, earthy brand of humor that found immediate favor among Americans.

This is not to say that the other pioneering cartoonists were sobersides. The revenge of James Akin reflects the salty humor that sometimes turned up. Akin, a Carolinian, at the age of thirty-one turned up in Massachusetts and did some map and chart engraving for Edmund Blunt, publisher of *Blunt's Coast Pilot.* In a quarrel over a detail, Blunt hurled a heavy iron skillet at Akin. Within a few days, Akin published a spirited caricature of Blunt's deed, which, as intended, discomfited Blunt. Akin pushed his revenge further. He sent a print to England to be reproduced by a maker of crockery on pitchers, washbowls, and chamber pots. These were imported in large numbers into Massachusetts, especially the last item. Most were bought up and destroyed by Blunt and his friends. The few that survived are prized collectors items.

Amos Doolittle, who was widely known for crude engravings of the battle of Lexington in 1775, numbered among his cartoons on the War of 1812 a rare bit of fastasy and remarkable brevity. It shows an animal, half bull half peacock, sounding "Boo-O-O-O-hoo," while it is stung in the neck by an enormous hornet, which is saying "Free trade and sailors' rights you old rascal!"

William Charles is considered by some historians to be the first real American practitioner of the cartoon. He produced a large volume of work and it had the widest circulation of any cartoonist's. Charles was an able engraver and found plenty of work in the States after he left Scotland. He turned out a number of English fairy tales with whimsical engravings and art for pamphlets. Charles borrowed heavily from the English, especially Rowlandson, but was not without a certain originality, especially his brand of humor. Nothing will establish a cartoonist faster than a successful picture called "The Present State of the Country"—a theme popular with cartoonists today. This is the title of a cartoon by Charles that makes the point that partisan disunity over the War of 1812 threatens the nation's existence. The prowar Jeffersonian on one side is attacking the pillar of Federalism; the antiwar Federalist on the other side is trying to pull down the pillar of Democracy. The spirit of Washington warns them that the nation's welfare depends on both pillars and a third for Republicanism. The theme strikes a modern note, the need for unity,

John Bull being stung by the Wasp and Hornet in a cartoon by Amos Doolittle.

and even the treatment is less cluttered than most. Another well-conceived but badly drawn Charles cartoon suggests that true American sailors put patriotism over safety and profits. Three sturdy sailors in a tavern scorn a ragged little Federalist newspaper editor, urging them to resist the embargo. The wordy balloons express their scorn, for "who would mutiny 'gainst commander and desert ship 'cause a hard gale and a tough passage brings him to short allowance." The victories of American Captain Oliver Perry over the British in Lake Erie inspired Charles to a punning cartoon common at the time. It shows a character combining John Bull and King George III getting a "Dose of Perry," a reference to both the naval victor and *perry,* the drink made from pear juice that made people run to the bathroom frequently. The same pun turns up in an Amos Doolittle cartoon, "Brother Jonathan administering a healthful cordial to John Bull," the cordial being labeled "Perry."

In another cartoon, the Russian bear is attempting to mediate between America and a chastened John Bull, but America, in flowing robe and holding stars and stripes, expresses concern over John Bull's horns. The darkest political moment of the war came in 1814, when representatives of Massachusetts, Connecticut, and Rhode Island met at Hartford to discuss seceding. The amused contempt of the rest of the country was expressed in a cartoon by Charles. He shows the three New England states on a ledge but shrinking from a step that presented too many risks. Below the ledge are King George III with open arms and Timothy Pickering, a secessionist leader, praying he will be made an English lord. No point is driven home just once when it can be driven

An 1812 Amos Doolittle cartoon about Brother Jonathan and John Bull.

home twice or more. A tablet on the ledge is inscribed with the names of heroes of the war. Another cartoon by Charles depicts with skilled bias the British who burned Washington as pillagers and the Washingtonians as cowards. Finally, in 1815, came a great American victory at New Orleans. It was the final battle of the war, actually fought two weeks after a peace agreement had been reached. Charles shows John Bull as a thick-bodied lout, his wig gone, being pulled out of a New Orleans swamp by American riflemen. The cartoon expresses what the nation felt. Americans, badly pummeled by the British throughout the war, could at last savor a great—if meaningless—victory.

CHAPTER V

WITH the end of the War of 1812 came what the *Columbian Centinel* early in James Monroe's presidency called the "era of good feelings." Only it wasn't. On the surface, it was a period of peace, of soaring nationalism, a period in which the country's character took shape. The Federalists had committed suicide as a party and the nation was in a period of one-party rule. A surge of national pride covered old political differences. But beneath the surface, the national currents were turbulent. On the surface there was Monroe, the last President to wear an old-style cocked hat. He straddled the bygone era of Washington and the Founding Fathers and the new age of nationalism and militant Americanism. Underneath the tranquility and prosperity were grave economic issues, and the conflict over slavery was beginning to raise its ugly head.

Not only the country's character but the characters that symbolize the country took shape in this period. During the War of 1812 Amos Doolittle had done a cartoon of a figure that was to evolve into Uncle Sam. In a cartoon already mentioned, Brother Jonathan—a tall, sturdy fisherman or a farmer, simple but shrewd, representing America—is forcing a tankard of perry down the throat of John Bull after Perry's naval victory. The cartoonist wrote that it was done to "inspire our countrymen with confidence in themselves and eradicate any terrors they may feel as respects the enemy they have to combat." It sold wholesale for seven dollars per hundred when purchased in lots of a hundred, which seems a bargain indeed, considering what it was supposed to do. No one really knows how the Brother Jonathan figure emerged, but it is believed that the name, Brother Jonathan, was a mildly derisive epithet used by the loyalists in the Revolution to refer to the rebels, and then became a name for the Americans used by the Americans themselves.

The name Uncle Sam is also believed to have appeared as a result of the War of 1812, although again, no one knows for sure. Most agree that it stems from the initials "U.S." stamped on the containers of government supplies by Samuel Wilson of Troy, New York, who was known locally as "Uncle Sam." It got about that "Uncle Sam" was feeding and taking care of the Army. From that time on, Uncle Sam began to represent the collective American household. The noted historian, Allan Nevins, thought Uncle Sam a disgrace, a "crude stereotype" that did not do justice to the nation. But out of their collective genius America's political cartoonists created Uncle Sam, the symbol of the nation, and shaped and reshaped him to the Uncle Sam of today. Americans have taken to Uncle Sam as their symbol, a symbol just as familiar to the Russians or Chinese it is to us. Cartoonist Rollin Kirby once said: "It would be difficult to manage a daily cartoon without him."

The first known cartoon of Uncle Sam is in a lithograph of 1832 that shows him as a sick man in a striped robe and nightcap, surrounded by quack doctors, all political figures, including Andrew Jackson and Martin Van Buren. Several years later, a cartoon, "Uncle Sam with La Grippe," shows an older man in a robe of stars and stripes being tended by the same political figures. The patient is irritable and wants to call in Dr. Biddle, head of the United States Bank, for his ailments. Outside, Brother Jonathan is welcoming Biddle. It is the only time Uncle Sam and Brother Jonathan are pictured together. Perhaps Brother Jonathan was conceived as the people and Uncle Sam as the United States. By 1840, Uncle Sam had acquired the now traditional top hat and striped pants, but not the whiskers. A woodcut shows him chasing two pups with the faces of Jackson and Van Buren.

The era of good feelings blew up with a bang in 1824. For twenty years the presidential nomination had been passed around by the Republicans, but now there were too many candidates, including Andrew Jackson, John Quincy Adams, and Henry Clay, the powerful Speaker of the House. Jackson got a plurality (the most votes) but not a majority. Following the provisions in the Constitution, the election was thrown into the House of Representatives. Clay decided on John Quincy Adams, and Adams got the plum—the presidency. Masses of angered Jacksonians, most of them common folks, screamed foul. In 1828, Jackson got his revenge and swept into the presidency.

The first election cartoon in the United States was

UNCLE SAM'S PET PUPS!
Or, Mother BANK'S last refuge.
Sold at ELTON'S, 18 Division-Street, New-York.

An 1840 woodcut depicting Uncle Sam in top hat and striped pants. The "pups" are Jackson and Van Buren.

inspired by the 1824 election and was created by David Claypoole Johnson, one of the nation's foremost artists of the pre–Civil War period. He was good at both cartooning and caricature, and his humorous work led to his being called the American Cruikshank. The cartoon shows three of the leading candidates, Adams, Jackson, and William H. Crawford, Monroe's Treasury Secretary, toeing the mark at the starting line. Behind them, Henry Clay, the fourth leading candidate, is hesitating about entering the race or not—indecision characteristic of his long political career. John Adams is waving a cocked hat, encouraging his son "Jack" (John Quincy Adams). A man from the West next to him is shouting, "Hurrah for our

Jack-son." The remarks of the backers and onlookers that make up the cheering, jeering crowd in the background are shot through with such puns. The background is filled with balloons of comment and a slimmed-down version of the capitol. Adams was considered the "safe" candidate. Crawford had the political connections. Clay had the most clearly defined program. Jackson, the hero of the victory at New Orleans, represented the democratic spirit of the frontier. The cartoon reflects what was happening: never before had the country taken such interest in the choice of the President. In every state, meeting after meeting was held. The people favored "Old Hickory" Jackson; they formed Hickory Clubs and carried hickory poles. One reason Clay threw the election to Adams was that he thought Adams would be unpopular and he—Clay—would be a shoo-in to succeed him. But Clay became Secretary of State under Adams. It had the smell of a deal and made Jackson the most popular man in the country.

Along with the "triumph of the common man" that marked a turning point in the nation's history, there were turning points in the 1830's in the reproduction of cartoons that are vignettes of the nation's triumphs and trials. Until then, all cartoons in America were engraved, etched, or cut on steel, copper, or wood, as they had been for hundreds of years. In etching, a print was made from a copper plate that was either smoked or covered with varnish or wax. The artist could cut directly into the copper or scratch through only the varnish. If he scratched the varnish, acid was poured over the plate, biting through the exposed part, eating out the lines not protected by the coating. For printing, ink was spread on the plate, then wiped off except where it filled the etched lines. When a special damp paper is put over the plate and the two are run through a press, the result is the transfer of the image on the plate onto the paper. In making an engraving, the engraver cuts his picture directly into a metal plate with special tools. The woodcut, a form of engraving, was the first popular type of print. An image was cut into the surface of a block of wood with special knives, ink was rubbed on the surface, and paper pressed against the damp surface. Great artists such as Brueghel, Rembrandt, Hogarth, Goya, and Daumier are among those whose prints are art treasures.

From the 1830's on, the lithographic process began to be the most popular means of graphic reproduction, and there was soon a flood of lithographs—portraits, pretty views, and cartoons. Lithography is an inexpensive method of reproduction that avoids going through the long, costly process of engraving on metal. Lithography is based on a simple scientific principle well known in every kitchen—that oil or grease and water do not mix. The artist makes the picture on white or gray flat limestone, using a wax crayon to draw the design. The stone is bathed in water mixed with gum arabic. Then, over the stone is rolled an oil-based ink that sticks only to the areas that have been covered by the wax crayon. The ink has no chemical affinity for the wax-free areas. A faithful impression of the drawing can then be transferred to paper from the moistened stone. Scores of impressions can be taken off a stone in this manner, for the process reproduces perfectly every small detail and variation of the original drawing.

The early decades of the 1800's also saw the beginning

of humorous illustration and social caricature. The rise of temperance groups prompted cartoons poking fun at them. The opening illustration to *The New Quizzical Valentine Writer* shows a dancing demon frightening an old maid by thrusting at her a pair of pants on a stick. The side-splitting humor is helped along by these four lines:

Fear not, fair Virgin, free from Sin;
This Present from your Friend I bring,
Which if refused, you know full well,
Apes you must shortly lead in Hell."

The social caricature that emerged at the time in a flurry of pamphlets and single sheets was characterized by a gross, robust sense of humor and poor quality of art and production. The titles of the works give an indication of what was considered humor in this genre at the time: *The Galaxy of Wit or Laughing Philosopher; The Aurora Borealis, or Flashes of Wit; Elton's Comic All-My-Neck; Broad Grins; The John Donkey; Yankee Doodle; The Rip Snorter.* The appearance of the great English humor magazine, *Punch,* in 1841 inspired a number of tawdry American imitations—among them *Punchinello, American Punch,* and *Southern Punch,* most of which never went beyond the first issue. In the early decades of the 1800's people had their comics. In the closing decades of the 1900's we wonder what was so funny. A century from now, people will be asking the same question about today's comics.

CHAPTER VI

ANDREW Jackson's election to the presidency has been called the revolution of 1828; it was to a large extent the climax of a forty-year struggle for people's right to vote. Under the Federalists, the state legislatures, not the citizens, voted for the President. America was ruled by a select few, an oligarchy of brains and wealth, whether aristocratic Federalist merchants or aristocratic Jeffersonian planters. But by 1828, new Western states and some of the old ones had granted citizens the vote. Jackson's victory—his supporters gloried in the name "Democrats"—speeded the transfer of power from the counting house to the farmhouse, westward from the conservative Eastern seaboard. If Jefferson was the hero of the gentleman farmer, Jackson was the hero of the dirt farmer. Jackson, the "people's candidate," was the man of the Western frontiersmen and the Eastern laborers, the personification of the new democratic spirit.

The first American cartoon produced by the new process of lithography depicted the new America. It is unique in conception and content, though poorly executed and dependent on balloons scattered all over. It is called "A New Map of the United States, With the Additional Territories." The map shows the eastern United States from Maine to Arkansas, including the organized territories of Florida, Michigan, and Arkansas, and the unorganized territory north and west of Missouri. But across the country, roped tail to tail, are an alligator and a tortoise. The man-eating alligator represents the Jacksonian Democrats of the West. A song of the time, "The Hunters of Kentucky," celebrated the prowess of the backwoods Kentuckians and Tennesseans as being "half horse, half alligator." The tortoise represents the conservative immobile party of John Quincy Adams that Jackson crushed. Figures atop each creature utter some of the political catchphrases of the day. But more interesting is the top part of the lithograph, showing "A view of the Rocky Mountains as surveyed by a company of Winnebago Indians." A party of Winnebagos has recently visited the East. One has seen ballet dancers, and, according to the balloons, says he can "teach our squaws now to show their legs without impropriety." Others have acquired enough English to say "A-dam No-a! Jack-son Ou-rah!" The cartoon, perhaps the work of an unknown amateur, is intriguing not only as a first but as a graphic representation of the political tug of war at the time.

It is an unanswered question whether the flood of distinctively American cartoons that began with and covered the Jackson presidency (1828–1836) was the result of the new, simple, and cheap method of lithographic reproduction or of the grave issues and the interest in Old Hickory's actions. But there is no question that political cartoons began to have mass appeal. Lithograph cartoons, published on separate sheets, were exceedingly popular. The sheets, varying in size from ten by twelve inches to fourteen by twenty inches, retailed for about twelve to twenty-five cents apiece. Most are anonymous, lacking either the cartoonist's or publisher's name— probably an action of discretion. Two elements to make cartoons a mass medium came together when cost came down and a subject colorful and controversial enough turned up: lithography and Jackson.

Jackson was a natural for cartoonists of any age or political persuasion. He was a new kind of President. He was no intellectual, no aristocrat, no political philosopher, no diplomat like his predecessors. He personified the new West: its individualism, its jack-of-all-trades versatility, its opportunism. He was a genuine folk hero. He was the first President to come from a log cabin, the first except Washington without a college education. While he had risen from the masses, he was not one of them. He was essentially a frontier aristocrat, owning many slaves and living in one of the finest mansions of America, the Hermitage in Tennessee. All through his presidency, Jackson was an unfailing storm center.

Jackson began his presidency by introducing a practice that one of his supporters in Congress blandly justified with "to the victor belongs the spoils." The Democrats cleaned out many Federalist office holders, saying "the barnacles shall be scraped clean from the ship of state," and replaced them with Republicans. Then Jackson got caught up in a tempest of petticoat politics that wrecked his Cabinet. Rumors of a scandalous past clung to the wife of Jackson's friend and Secretary of War, John Eaton, and the wives of other Cabinet officers, led by the wife of Vice-president John C. Calhoun, snubbed her. Jackson, whose own wife had been done to death by scandalmongers, went to bat for Peggy Eaton. Secretary of State Martin Van Buren and Eaton left the Cabinet voluntarily; the others were kicked out. Van Buren, who upheld Peggy Eaton's honor, became in Jackson's eyes the gallant champion of a woman's virtue and his closest adviser. Calhoun was the big loser; he got bumped as the heir to Jackson.

The war over Peggy intrigued cartoonists. One of the most effective cartoons was "The Rats Leaving a Falling House," by Edward William Clay. It shows rats with the faces of the Cabinet members leaving the collapsing Jackson house. Jackson's foot is pinning down the tail of the Van Buren rat. It made such an impact that when Van Buren's son was asked if his father would return to his home state of New York, he replied—without puzzling anyone—"When the President takes off his foot."

The trifling episode was the beginning of a break between Calhoun, a supporter of states' rights, and Jackson, which was expressed in an exchange of toasts at a dinner. Jackson's toast was "Our Union: it must be preserved." Calhoun responded: "The Union, next to our liberty." In Jackson's first term, an old and frightening issue came up. Could a state refuse to enforce federal laws in its territory? South Carolina declared federal tariffs null and void. In support of nullification, the collection of tariff fees would be halted. The real leader of the nullifiers was Calhoun. Jackson prepared to lead troops against his native state. As a first step, he announced he

"The Rats Leaving a Falling House," by Edward William Clay.

would try Calhoun for treason and "hang him as high as Haman." Henry Clay, the "Great Compromiser," eventually worked out a compromise. Years later, when asked if he had any regrets in his life, Jackson said he had two: he had been unable to shoot Henry Clay or to hang John C. Calhoun. In contrast to the relative simplicity of the "Cabinet rats" cartoon there is a lithograph that attempts to depict the nullification issue symbolically, in the grand manner. It shows Calhoun at the top of a series of steps, the bottom one labeled "Nullification" and the top one "Disunion," reaching for the crown of "Despotism." President Jackson is holding back Calhoun's supporters, threatening, "I'll hang you all." Another well-drawn cartoon uses the concept of a huge pie filled with eggs bearing the initials of the states, with a broken one on top, "South Carolina," and, standing by, an amusing John Bull as a greedy boy, knife and fork in hand, eager to get something good out of nullification. One of the rare newspaper cartoons of the period showing the other side of the argument depicts the North and South as Siamese twins, but the South is bending under a heavy burden of "Tariff Taxes." Along with the cartoon was an editorial supporting nullification. The paper was put out in the nation's capital, of all places.

To many Americans, Jackson was a dictator and a tyrant, destroying American liberties, just as to many others he was a defender of the common man and a foe of privilege. These conflicting views gave rise to a number of cartoons. One of the best of the anti-Jackson cartoons, in drawing skill and production, depicts "King Andrew the First." Jackson, in royal robes, is trampling on the

"Despotism—Anarchy—Disunion" depicting Jackson at right and Calhoun reaching for the crown.

An unknown artist depicts President Jackson as "King Andrew the First" in 1832.

Constitution and on Supreme Court decisions. Americans fought a revolution to get rid of the king, and this cartoon is one of the first to use the king as a symbol of the bad, a symbol that appears again and again in the nation's political cartoons. Another anti-Jackson cartoon, realistic and most unusual because it shows only two figures instead of an assembly and has no balloons, shows Henry Clay sewing up Jackson's mouth. The point was that the Senate, prodded by Clay, had passed a resolution of censure charging Jackson with arrogating to himself unconstitutional power. Jackson fired back an enraged protest message, but Clay prevented the blast from being entered into the record. While Clay—and the cartoon—could give Jackson the needle, it took more than needlework to hold him down. The spirited cartoon, like the "Rats" cartoon, so uncharacteristic of the times by not being gussied up, is by the same cartoonist, David Claypoole Johnson.

The biggest fright of the Jackson presidency, which was accompanied by scores of cartoons, was the battle over the "moneyed monster" known as the Bank of the United States. Once again, Clay, aspiring to the presidency, was pitted against Jackson. Although called a "national bank," the bank was really a private corporation with a monopoly on government deposits and the nation's currency and credit. It was headed by Nicholas Biddle, a Philadelphia patrician, who once said, "I have been for years with more personal authority than any President." Clay, Daniel Webster, and other anti-Jackson men pushed through a bill for an early renewal of the bank's charter. Jackson vetoed it, calling the bank un-

American, undemocratic, and unconstitional. He summed up the complex financial issues in these words: "Shall the rights of the common man be respected or shall the rich rule the country again?" Jackson ordered the withdrawal of all government deposits from the bank.

Most cartoonists—and the people—applauded the President's action. One cartoon shows the pillars of the bank collapsing and Biddle and his men scurrying for their lives. By Jackson's side, cheering, is Jack Downing, a kind of Uncle Sam character who didn't survive. Another cartoon shows Jackson slaying the "many-headed monster." The monster's biggest head is Biddle's. Jack Downing is lending a helping hand. Another shows Jackson, in a nightmare, fighting the thrashing dragon-bank. In another cartoon the bank is shown as a sick old lady, spewing up money while Biddle holds "Mother Bank's" head. Drs. Clay, Webster, and Calhoun consult as to what to do. Jackson and Jack Downing are peeping through a window with pleasure. There are many other cartoons in the same vein, and Jack Downing turns up in a goodly number, as a kind of comic philosopher who speaks the mind of the man in the street. The bank, the only national financial institution in the nation's history, had many advantages, but it was, as charged, a "hydra of corruption," with many congressmen getting "loans" from it. And it was run by an arrogant wealthy clique. The withdrawal of the government's deposits sealed the bank's doom. It was crushed, and Henry Clay, long bitten by the presidential bug but no longer with big money on his side, also was crushed. The Jackson years were full of noise and bluster and bull-in-the-china-shop policies, but

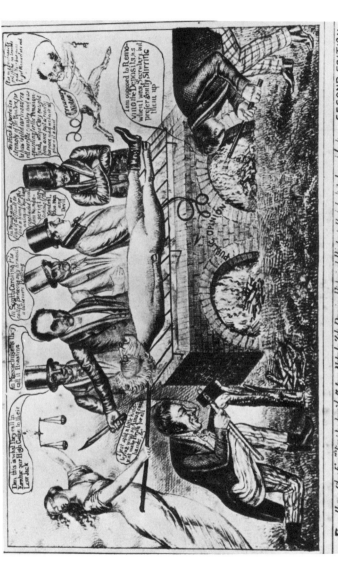

This 1832 cartoon shows Andrew Jackson on the grill of public opinion. The first three figures behind him, starting at the left, are Henry Clay, Daniel Webster, and John Calhoun.

it was also a time of a strong President, a time for the common people to become part of the political process, and a time when the two major parties became the Democrats and the Whigs. It was also the time when the political cartoon began to flourish.

CHAPTER VII

PROBABLY no President has ever been so frequently and bitterly attacked by cartoonists as was Jackson. Among the Presidents who came after him, up to the Civil War, James Buchanan ran Jackson a close second for the unenvied honor. Most of the others, relatively obscure in their times, remain obscure to this day. Of course, Lincoln had more than a fair share of the cartoon attacks, and asking who got knocked most may be splitting hairs.

The time between Jackson and Lincoln was for the most part filled with Presidents who made no great mark on the course of American history. Even historians have a hard time recalling whether Tyler came before Taylor or vice versa, and who was in between. It was a time when education for all—even women—became a democratic ideal. A native American literature began to be created by writers like James Fenimore Cooper, Henry David Thoreau, Ralph Waldo Emerson, Washington Irving, Henry Wadsworth Longfellow, and Edgar Allan Poe. American ports prospered from ocean commerce. Machines and the factory system were bringing on the Industrial Revolution. New machines were changing American farming. Miners and settlers were moving into Western lands. The era of Manifest Destiny, when most Americans believed the entire continent was destined to be theirs, was beginning to take form. The nation acquired Texas, New Mexico, California, Oregon. And there was over all the ominous shadow of another destiny, foreshadowed by the revolt of slaves led by Nat Turner and the rise of the abolitionists. The country remained lulled as the slavery issue moved from crisis to compromise to crisis to compromise, until finally it ran out of compromise and faced what had become inevitable—civil war.

With the cartoonists no longer as active in the political arena as in Jackson's day, there was a profusion of what today would be called comic books; in those days they were called almanacs. Some were westerns or were about sports and they had titles similar to specialized magazines of today. The first was *The American Comic Almanac,* which contained jokes and crude pictures. It caught on and was followed by a host of imitators during the years of the Jackson presidency and that of his successor, Martin Van Buren, and went on for years, nearly to the Civil War. Among the first comic almanacs on the scene were *The Comic Token, The American Comic Annual, Finn's Comic Almanac,* and *Fisher's Comic Almanac.* Because the woodcut illustrations were crude, the textual matter heavy-handed, and the humor simple, the inclusion of the word *comic* in every title was probably a useful guide to the reader that the intent was to be funny. The readers found them so: they enjoyed the rough-and-ready and down-to-earth humor. And they could always look at the illustrations, in many instances much funnier than the words. *Davy Crockett's Almanac of Wild Sports of the West and Life in the Backwoods* was started in Tennessee in 1835, the year before Crockett died, and continued under various publishers until 1856. The tales and jokes were in dialect, with each issue full of the tall stories that matched Crockett's words in the first issue: "I can run faster, jump higher, squat lower, dive deeper, stay under water longer and come out drier than any man in the whole country." There are, however, some striking graphic sketches illustrating Colonel Crockett's definitions, in dialect, of a sucker, of a puke—"the most all-sickenin' ugly critters from Uncle Sam's twenty-six states"—of a Hoosier and a Wolverine. The last is described in part in this way:

The chaps from the Wolverine State are the all-greediest, ugliest, an sourest characters on all Uncle Sam's farms, they are, in thar natur, like their wildish namesakes, always so eternal hungry that they bite at the air and hang their underlips and show the narrow teeth of their mouths as if they'd jump right into you an swallow you hull, without salt.

Some of the other almanacs left off the word *comic* but made up for it with names like *Whim Whams, The Rip Snorter,* and *The Merry Elephant* and catchall combinations like *The Devil's Comical Texas Oldmanick.* An even more mouth-filling combination was *The Genius of Comedy, or Life in New York, a Ludico-Comico Medley* of 1830, possibly one of the first humor magazines in the United States. But it may have been matched in 1836 by *The Salmagundi and News of the Day—A Comical, Satirical, Hu-*

morous and Entertaining Journal of Scraps & Engravings, all on a jumbo newsprint sheet.

While there was now a little less fire in the political cartoons that dominated the American scene—targets like Jackson do not come along that frequently—there was a beginning of social satire and social commentary in the years after Old Hickory. There was, for example, a prediction of the end of the world that, then as today, set the ink in the cartoonists' pens flowing. In the 1840's, William Miller led Adventist preachers in predicting the world would be "cleansed by fire" on April 23, 1843. For weeks people disposed of all they had and gathered in huge tents on hillsides to await doom. This provoked a small lithograph of a large fireproof safe with the key on the inside of the door. The safe is stocked with ice, cheese, cigars, a ham, and a palmleaf fan. Seated on the safe's floor is a man thumbing his nose and saying, "Now let it come! I'm ready!" In 1849 gold was discovered in California. The rush of 80,000 Americans on an ill-considered trek westward was more tragic than funny. But there was whimsy in some of the unbelievable characters among the forty-niners, and the cartoonists saw it. One cartoon, labeled "Off for California," shows a scene at the dock, which is crowded with forty-niners, weeping wives, and lawmen with warrants. The gold seekers, some wearing top hats, are bent over with excess baggage. In contrast to the hubbub of that scene is the serene, solitary fellow depicted in "A Gold Hunter on His Way to California." His equipment includes high boots, a pick, a shovel, a pan, a pair of balances, a tea-kettle, a string of sausages, a pocketful of knives and pistols, an iron pot serving as a helmet, and a luggage bag. He is passing with unconcern a signpost that says "St. Louis 350 miles; California 1,700 miles."

The Americans of the 1840's—17 million—were bursting with energy and self-esteem. They danced polkas and read lots of books. Women's rights were furthered by Amelia Bloomer's invention of the female pants that were named for her. "Humbug" was Americans' response to being suckered in by P. T. Barnum as they flocked to his shows. Railroads crisscrossed the East and headed toward the Mississippi. In the cities, horse-drawn omnibuses were in use. Inventions included the telegraph, ether anesthesia, rubber-soled shoes, air conditioning, and an automatic egg-hatching machine. It was a period of pride, and the pride was reflected in the lithographs of the time. Of these, the best known are those of Currier & Ives, prints that once sold for six cents apiece wholesale and are now part of the treasured American heritage. The firm, started by Nathaniel Currier, who grew up with lithography, became Currier & Ives when James Ives joined it as a partner. At its peak, Currier & Ives so far outstripped its competitors as to leave them virtually forgotten. The firm produced nearly 8,000 prints, using a number of artists, many of whom became famous in their own right. The firm produced political cartoons, generally well-mannered. Among them is the first print of the political activities of what today would be called feminism. There was a long series of prints devoted to views of America. There were portraits that pictured the great figures of the United States and other countries. There were historical prints, many of them copies of original paintings. There were sentimental prints—of partings, returns, love and marriage—filled with moral, religious, and uplifting moments and thoughts. There were prints for children, Mississippi River prints, railroad prints, ship prints, horse prints, sporting prints and comic prints. The small prints were sold for fifteen to twenty-five cents apiece; larger ones retailed for one-fifty to three dollars each. The firm, based in New York, sold prints all over the country and in Britain, France, and Europe. The firm issued a number of catalogues regularly, much in the same manner that book publishers put out "trade lists" today.

Starting with the first great best seller, "The Extra Sun," a lithograph picturing a steamboat that caught fire on Long Island Sound with the loss of many lives—produced within several days of the disaster—the Currier & Ives prints combined skilled craftsmanship, artistic talent, and smart merchandising with the keenest news sense of the day. The "rush" prints, depicting events and persons in the news, sold fabulously and made the firm an institution. It launched the firm of Currier & Ives, which considered itself a publisher of "Colored Engravings for the People," on a long career that depicted with fidelity and imagination every phase of life in a country that was growing from adolescence to maturity.

The Currier & Ives prints, which made their way into nearly every home, covered so much that no taste was left unsatisfied. Prints depicted the land and naval battles of the Mexican and Civil wars, clipper ships and whalers, railroads and fire scenes, disasters and wrecks, Presidents and pugilists and such notables as Barnum's General Tom Thumb, panoramic views of cities and farm and country life, life among the Indians, the winning of the West, and countless other subjects as varied and as

73

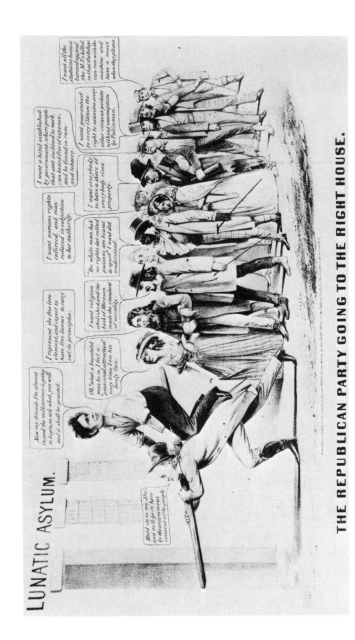

THE REPUBLICAN PARTY GOING TO THE RIGHT HOUSE.

An anti-Lincoln lithograph of Currier & Ives in 1860, drawn by Louis Maurer.

colorful as America itself. The entire collection of prints forms a great panoramic picture of mid-eighteenth-century America. Today, some prints look crude, quaint, moralistic, and melodramatic, but most are the work of accomplished and talented artists, who produced colorful, accurate representations of the era. Currier & Ives pictured its own times with meticulous accuracy of detail, without "artiness" and with no thought of appealing to any but their own contemporaries. It gave the public pictures that were easy to understand and appreciate, pictures that were typically American, pictures about things within the knowledge and experience of the average person—all at a price within the range of the average pocketbook. No era in history has been more fortunate in its portrayers.

CHAPTER VIII

MARTIN Van Buren, the eighth President of the United States, was the first to be born under the American flag. It was Andrew Jackson's will that Van Buren, his friend and his vice president, be his successor. A smart politician with wide experience in government, Van Buren was called "a first-class second-rate man." Jackson gave his man powerful help so that he won easily, but he also willed him a deep economic depression. Van Buren was hardly in office when he inherited bad times, in part because of Jackson's bank policies. He never got out from under the depression doldrums.

The first appearance of a donkey in connection with the Democrats appeared when Van Buren took over from Jackson and the banking system of the country was falling to pieces. It is in a cartoon showing Jackson riding the donkey, using a whip labeled with the Jackson actions that had furthered the economic chaos. Van Buren is walking behind him. In the donkey's path are the ghosts of bankruptcies; in the background are the doors of closed banks. Two cartoons by Edward Williams Clay treat the

The first appearance of the Democratic donkey. Andrew Jackson is riding it.

same theme. One shows a planter and laborer upholding the Democrats as they sit on one side of a table. On the other side is the ghost of the dead business of the nation giving Van Buren statistics of the financial disaster. Presiding is Jackson wearing a stars-and-stripes apron and looking like a shrew. Jackson's hand is propping up Van Buren; tucked in his apron is a bowie knife to keep Van Buren in line. The other cartoon is called "The Times" and shows jobless workers without shoes, women and children begging, a closed factory, and a run on a bank, while saloons and pawnshops prosper.

Hard times did Van Buren in, and he never made it to a second term. The opposition Whigs—a name borrowed from the patriots of the Revolution—won with a military figure famed for a victory at Tippecanoe in 1811. The Whigs stole the Democrats' thunder. Since Jackson had won by appealing to the common man, the Whigs announced they were common men too. One reason the military man, General William Henry Harrison, was picked by the Whigs to run was that no one knew where he stood and he never said a single word about what he thought or what he would do. The general, at sixty-eight, was the oldest man to become President until the election of Ronald Reagan in 1980. His running mate was an aristocratic Virginia conservative, John Tyler. The Whig election slogan thus became "Tippecanoe and Tyler too." Harrison was from one of the first families of Virginia and lived in a mansion in a vast estate, but the Whigs got help from an anti-Harrison newspaper story that said the general was hard up and would be content with hard cider, a pension, and his log cabin. Gleefully picking up the idea, they created a fantasy candidate, publicizing

Harrison as a farmer in a log cabin. It was the first introduction of modern publicity techniques in the staid presidential campaigns. The Whigs flooded the country with cartoons, stories, and songs and parades about Old Tippecanoe and his imaginary log cabin.

One lithograph shows Harrison in simple buckskins standing by a plow pulled by a horse as he greets Van Buren and other Democratic leaders, all dandied up for a visit to his farm. Two lithographs by Edward Williams Clay deal with another ploy, the cider barrel. One shows the Democrats tripping over a cider barrel and tumbling down toward a log cabin. Another shows Van Buren in his nightclothes running out of the White House, upset by a dream he was being crushed in a cider press. Another cartoonist shows Harrison greeting a one-legged ex-soldier in front of a tiny cabin with two cider barrels along the side. The cabin even has a flagpole and an American flag. Another shows a cider barrel as a steam locomotive plowing into Van Buren's wagon. There were endless variations on the theme, plus numerous Harrison almanacs picturing a cabin and cider barrels.

Other cartoons took another tack: a boxing match between Van Buren and Harrison, with the two slugging away with bare knuckles. It was one of the earliest political cartoons in which the candidates are drawn as boxers. A Western frontiersman is seconding Harrison; Jackson is seconding Van Buren. The sports motif became as predictable as the use of puns by cartoonists, especially puns on people's names. From 1832 to 1864, every four years the candidates vied for the presidency in a sports contest. Another cartoon showed a game of pool between Harrison and Van Buren, with the ever present Jackson by Van Buren's side. In 1844, "Political Cockfighters" shows Henry Clay and James Polk pitted against one another. "The Race Course" shows Clay and Polk in a contest over a water course. An 1848 cartoon shows Zachary Taylor in a card game with his rival candidates. In 1852 Pierce has the lead in a footrace for the presidency. Baseball players Lincoln and three rivals are shown in an 1860 cartoon entitled "The National Game. Three 'Outs' and One 'Run.'" In 1864, "A Little Game of Bagatelle Between the Rail Splitter and Little Mac, the Gunboat General" pictures Lincoln, seeking a second term, in a contest with General George McClellan at the bagatelle table. This is just a sampling of diverse sports and games used to portray contending presidential candidates.

The Van Buren–Harrison campaign added new expressions to the language. A cartoon shows Van Buren trying to head for a second term in the White House along a fork in a road blocked with log cabins and cider barrels. Van Buren looks somewhat longingly down another fork marked "To Kinderhook." Van Buren's home was called Kinderhook, and his nickname was "Old Kinderhook." The initials *O.K.* became an election slogan and ultimately took on the meaning they now have, "O.K." The Whigs rolled big balls of paper through city streets, a scene also picked up in lithographs. The Whigs chanted, "As rolls the ball Van's reign doth fall, and he may look to Kinderhook." They also sang, "It is the ball a-rolling for Tippecanoe and Tyler too." Out of this, "Keep the ball rolling" entered the language.

President Harrison, a Whig, liked to step out of the White House and buy his meat and vegetables. One

80

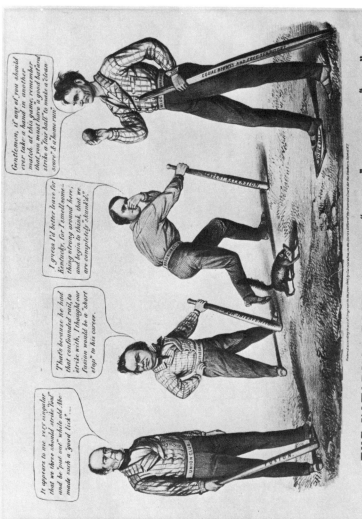

An 1860 Currier & Ives cartoon of Lincoln.

"Old Kinderhook," an 1840 woodcut of President Van Buren being pulled to the White House for a second term by Jackson.

morning he walked in the rain and caught a cold that developed into pneumonia. He died after thirty days in office, the shortest presidential tenure in American history. He was succeeded by John Tyler, the first "accidental" president. Tyler opposed many things the Whigs wanted and also had no use for the Jackson Democrats. The Whigs, furious at his high-handed scorn of their program, called him "His Accidency." The Democrats could hardly wait to defeat him. The Whigs drummed Tyler out of their party. He was the President nobody wanted. Not even the cartoonists showed interest in him; virtually no cartoons about him survive.

The first "dark horse" candidate and the first whose election was reported by telegraph was James Knox Polk, who succeeded the unwanted John Tyler. Polk was a protégé of the "godfather" of the Democrats, Andrew Jackson, and was known as "Young Hickory." He defeated Henry Clay, whom the Whigs finally nominated after his long years of being "ever a bridesmaid but never a bride." For the first and only time in American history, the man selected to run as vice-president (with Polk) refused the nomination. He was Silas Wright, who opposed annexing Western lands. Instead, George M. Dallas became Polk's running mate.

One of the key election issues was the matter of following through on Tyler's last-minute action and annexing Texas. Another was the boundary dispute over Oregon between Britain and the United States. These were vital issues because the question of extending slavery was intensifying: whether new states entered the Union as free states or slave states was a matter of bitter contention. Polk and the South were for annexing Texas; the Whigs

83

in the North were against it. Clay tried in his customary manner to straddle the fence. The antislavery abolitionists with their small party, the Liberty Party, influenced the election's outcome: their candidate took enough Whig votes away in New York to cost Clay the state, which in turn cost him the election and his last chance at the White House. All this was merely a curtain raiser that occurred before Polk even took office.

As Polk began his presidency, the Democratic editor of a New York newspaper gave Americans a dynamic new slogan when he wrote: "Our manifest destiny is to overspread and possess the whole of the continent which Providence has given us for the development of the great experiment of liberty and federated self-government entrusted to us." Polk fervently believed in this Manifest Destiny. To make sure, he pushed through the annexation of Texas, and he had his eye on an even greater prize—California. Nor was he soft-pedaling the American demand of "Fifty-four Forty or Fight," which meant the border of Oregon should go up to the Alaska border, at latitude fifty-four degrees and forty minutes. Polk compromised on the forty-ninth parallel in Oregon; to obtain California he maneuvered Mexico into a war after trying to buy New Mexico and California from Mexico. Generals Zachary Taylor and Winfield Scott led major compaigns in a war that lasted almost two years. Many of the younger officers would emerge soon in the spotlight of a greater war between Americans. When peace came, the United States had acquired Texas, the whole Southwest, California, and Western territory up to Oregon, increasing the total expanse of the United States by about two-thirds—an addition greater than that made by the Louisiana Purchase.

The events gave rise to a great many cartoons, but most were so full of characters and so cluttered with balloons full of the words of the characters that to describe them would take a set of books. One cartoon worthy of note shows Polk and other Democratic leaders doing a polka, the latest fashionable dance. The dance is described as "one step forward, two steps back," which is, of course, a perfect sardonic description of politics. Another cartoon shows Polk running to Texas and being butted by a woolly ram while the products of other industries that, like the wool industry, wanted protective tariffs shower upon his head. The cartoon could almost be used again in the 1980's by American automobile manufacturers seeking protection from the importing of cars from Japan. A cartoon by Edward Williams Clay, cluttered but imaginative, epitomizes Polk's commitment to Manifest Destiny and his obsession with the Oregon border issue. Called "Polk's Dream," it shows Polk confronted by a demonic apparition with Andrew Jackson's face, telling Polk "never to take your foot off that line should you deluge your country with seas of blood." Polk, on the fifty-four forty line on the Oregon map, vows to obey with a favorite Jacksonian expression, "By the Eternal." The cartoons inspired by the war with Mexico were overwhelmingly full of brag and jingoism. One with good comic effect shows the Mexican General Santa Anna with a spindly body, a grotesque head, and protruding eyes on an ambling nag, staring with astonishment at Zachary Taylor's army advancing to the Rio Grande. It was done

An Edward Williams Clay cartoon showing Polk and other Democratic leaders dancing a polka in 1844.

by one of the ablest cartoonists of the time, Napoleon Sarony. Probably the most "cutting" cartoon is another by Clay: Brother Jonathan strides across the Rio Grande to cut Mexico in two with a huge scissors, each blade part of Taylor's army. Brother Jonathan accuses Mexico of trying to steal Texas and says, "I'll discumgalligumfriate you."

The United States won the war, but quarrels over whether or not slavery should be allowed in the lands taken from Mexico started almost as soon as the war began. Militant Northerners opposed the creation of any new slave territories. Equally fiery Southerners demanded the right to take slaves into all new territories. A third view favored the doctrine of popular sovereignty—the people of each territory should themselves decide the issue of slavery or freedom. The moderates still outnumbered the extremists, but the "firebell" in Jefferson's mind that had alarmed him during the debate over Missouri's admission to the Union, years earlier, took on a more insistent, ominous ring.

CHAPTER IX

WITH the land gained from Mexico and the borders of Oregon and Maine settled, the United States stretched almost uninterrupted from the Atlantic to the Pacific. But it was not one country. In a sense, the opening shots of the Mexican War were the opening shots of the Civil War. President Polk, who was so worn out and ailing from his strenuous term in office that he died shortly after leaving office, left the nation the heritage of the golden West. But with the new lands came the heritage of an embittered and intensified dispute over slavery. Signs of the gathering and ever darkening storm over the nation can be read in two contrasting cartoons of the time. A proslavery cartoon published in New York shows a chilled and rejected free Negro in the North disconsolately nearing a saloon, while another panel of the cartoon shows a happy Southern slave sitting in the fields next to his white master, both smoking pipes. The evils of slavery from a Northern point of view are shown in a cartoon called "No Higher Law." King Slavery is seated on his throne holding aloft a lash and chain. By his elbow is a scroll, the Fugitive Slave Bill. His ministers are holding branding irons. Three slaves crouch by the throne, while beyond, a runaway slave is fighting off bloodhounds attacking him.

In the North, slavery had died out after the Revolutionary War because it was not profitable. Slavery had been declining in the South as well. The invention of the cotton gin in 1793 meant that almost overnight, short staple cotton became the dominant Southern crop. Slavery was reinvigorated, and the slaves became bound to the cotton gin and the planter bound to the slaves. The South became the cotton kingdom, a huge agricultural factory turning out avalanches of fluffy fiber. The planters, with booming profits, bought more slaves and land to grow more cotton so as to buy more slaves and land. Cotton came to be the largest and most vital export for the South.

The South even had foreign countries partially over a barrel. Britain was the leading industrial power, and its most important single manufacture was cotton cloth, supporting about a fifth of its population. Four-fifths of the fiber for the cotton cloth came from the South. Southern statesmen were fully aware that England was tied to them by cotton threads, and it gave them a heady sense of power in the conflict that was increasingly dividing the nation. Moreover, the South was less a democracy—in contrast to the rest of the country—than an oligarchy, a government of the few, dominated by a planter aristocracy. At one extreme, the Southerners made much of the "happy lot" of their blacks, and many Northerners were indifferent to the faraway Southern institution. Some people, like Abraham Lincoln, as a practical matter did not advocate abolishing slavery, but opposed its extension to new states. Finally, from the 1830's on, there was the other extreme, the abolitionists, as ardent and active against slavery as are the anti-nuclear protesters of today. They were disliked in the North and their importance overestimated by the South, but their zeal—matched by hotheaded Southern "fire-eaters"—added constant fuel to the spreading fire. The extreme groups helped destroy the relations between sections of the country, the good will that was the cement of the union. Men spoke the same language but no longer understood or regarded what the other said. Bonfires of hatred were lighted that in the end were only partially extinguished by buckets of blood.

President Polk, his goals mainly accomplished and his health broken, wanted only one term, so that in 1848 both parties were forced to seek new standard bearers. The Whigs turned to a war hero, General Zachary Taylor. His Mexican victories, his Southern birth, his ownership of 300 slaves, his clean political record—he'd never voted for anyone in his life—his undisclosed political views, if any, made him the best available candidate. When the Whigs mailed their nomination to him, he refused to pay the ten cents postage due and sent the letter back unopened. To oppose Taylor, the Democrats picked another general, Lewis Cass, an aged hero of the War of 1812. His enemies, referring to his pompousness, called him General Gass.

Both parties tried to avoid taking a stand on the new territories, but Cass's views were well known. He was the father of the doctrine of "popular sovereignty": the people living in a territory should decide the slavery issue themselves. Although it was an appealing doctrine, many feared it would serve to spread slavery. Ardent antislavery people in the North—Democrats who opposed the popular sovereignty idea, Whigs distrustful of both Taylor and Cass, and abolitionists—joined forces to form the Free-Soil party; their slogan was "Free soil, free speech, free labor and free men." The Free-Soilers took away enough votes from Cass in the crucial state of New York to throw the election to Taylor.

The election was a humdrum affair. Taylor inspired few favorable cartoons; one of the few shows the general's face as a cannonball knocking Cass into a cocked hat. There were far more anti-Taylor cartoons. One was entitled "An Available Candidate: The One Qualification for a Whig President." It depicts a smug, uniformed, and plumed Taylor enthroned on a pyramid of skulls, symbols of how Taylor had achieved fame. The cartoon was unlike any previous American political cartoon. Previous cartoons had been quite vicious, but most of the viciousness was in the balloons. In this case, however, the excellence of the artist made words unnecessary.

In 1850, Henry Clay, the Great Pacificator, then seventy-three years old, offered his last compromise: California was to be a free state; slavery in New Mexico and Utah would be decided by popular vote; a new and more stringent fugitive slave law would be passed. John C. Calhoun, who within weeks would die of tuberculosis, was bitterly opposed to this. Daniel Webster, also soon to die, countered by pleading for preservation of the Union. The debate represented the twilight of the three giants; it held the country spellbound.

In the midst of the stormy debate, President Taylor

died, stricken after a series of Fourth of July speeches under a broiling sun. He was succeeded by Millard Fillmore, a "doughface" President—"doughface" meaning a Northern politician with Southern ideas on slavery. It was first applied to Fillmore, the New Yorker who succeeded Taylor and soon ordered vigorous enforcement of the Fugitive Slave Act. This law, enacted as part of the Compromise of 1850, was for the South a symbol of the North's desire not to destroy the Union. For the North it was a pact with evil. It aroused a storm of opposition. So savage was the new law that it touched off an explosive chain reaction in the North. The Underground Railroad stepped up its activities to bring slaves from the South to freedom. Northern mobs rescued blacks being taken prisoner. Countless thousands in the North ceased to be moderate and passive about slavery. Thousands in the South became increasingly galled that the Yankees would not execute the law, the South's only real gain in the 1850 Compromise. Cartoons, which earlier had had fun with comic renditions of black amusements, turned bitter and vicious. But the most powerful influences were the words and drawings of the heart-tugging *Uncle Tom's Cabin*, by Harriet Beecher Stowe, whom President Lincoln once described as "the little woman who wrote the book that made this great war." Millions of copies were sold. It was quickly made into a play. When Simon Legree, villainous with his black mustache, his whips and bloodhounds—the dogs were featured chasing Eliza on cartoonlike theater posters—stalked across a thousand stages in the North, he personified the evils of slavery.

With no second term for President Fillmore, the Democrats, unable to agree on a candidate, finally picked the second dark horse in American history, Franklin Pierce. The Whigs, also deadlocked, finally went for the only type of winning candidate they had had in the past, a military hero. They turned to General Winfield Scott, "Old Fuss and Feathers," the ablest general of his time. Unhappy Northern Whigs broke away from the party. Pierce, the winner against a divided opposition, was also a doughface. The South ran Pierce's administration through his secretary of war, Jefferson Davis, the future president of the Confederacy. Under Pierce, the United States filled the last geographical gap by buying from Mexico what became the Kansas and Nebraska territories, with Nebraska to be a free state and Kansas a slave state.

But proslavery and antislavery bands fought a small-scale civil war over "Bleeding Kansas." A preamble to greater conflict that enflamed both North and South, it is depicted in a stark cartoon called "Liberty, the Fair Maid of Kansas in the Hands of Border Ruffians." The target is the Pierce administration for going along with the lawlessness. President Pierce and other key figures are in the foreground, grinning at the imploring Liberty, who is on her knees. In the background is depicted the slaughter in Kansas: men and women being shot, clubbed and stabbed. One of the most telling cartoons in American history was provoked by a speech delivered by Senator Charles Sumner of Massachusetts on "the crime against Kansas," blaming the South for the events and adding some snide remarks about the elderly Senator Andrew Butler of South Carolina. Three days later, Butler's nephew, Congressman Preston Brooks, walked up to Sumner in the Senate chamber, and beat him sense-

"Southern Chivalry" shows Preston Brooks trying to kill Senator Sumner.

less with a heavy cane. The cartoon, entitled "Southern Chivalry," depicts Sumner, still holding the quill he was using, on the floor, his feet tangled in his desk, while Brooks batters his skull. Behind them are senators, some laughing, none interfering. The cartoon has a concentrated graphic power the cartoonists of the day rarely showed. "Bully" Brooks became a hero in the South: admirers flooded him with canes. Senator Sumner was disabled for three years, but Massachusetts held his Senate seat for him. The North was mightily aroused over "Bleeding Kansas" and Brooks. Many cartoons echoed the outrage, but they were crude: for example, Brooks was shown in the stocks of Puritan times being pelted with vegetables and dead cats and dogs. The Sumner-

Brooks incident showed how inflamed people's minds were becoming as emotion displaced thought in both the North and South.

The fight over the Kansas-Nebraska issue disrupted the parties, splitting them into proslavery and antislavery factions and ultimately leading to the formation of a new party. The Republician party, the first truly sectional party, represented the interests of the Northeast and Northwest and was committed to opposing slavery. The party sprang up in many places in 1854 and soon won a good number of seats in Congress. In 1856 the Republicans made their first attempt to capture the presidency. Their candidate was a famous, glamorous explorer of the West, John C. Fremont. Sex appeal was directly brought into a presidential campaign for the first time when Fremont and his pretty wife, Jessie, daughter of a senator, appeared side by side in banners and cartoons. An antiforeigner, anti-immigrant party, known because of its secretiveness as the Know-Nothing Party, picked former President Fillmore. The Democrats picked James Buchanan, a bland, elderly diplomat uninvolved in the issues that were tearing the country apart. Buchanan was the victor and became the nation's last doughface president. He carried the South, but not the majority of the nation's voters. His victory was achieved by desperate efforts on the part of the Democratic machine to get votes and by the presence of the third party. For the Republicans it was a "victorious defeat."

The sex-appeal theme was captured in a cartoon that showed Old Buck (Buchanan was pronounced Buck-anan by many) slumped over a table, wrinkled and aged, and labeled "Old Fogyism," in contrast to "Young America" represented by the Fremonts. The campaign inspired much cartoon activity, but most cartoons were against Fremont. Many people were frightened by Southern threats to secede if he was elected. The moneyed and conservative elements backed Buchanan, branding members of the new party "Black Republicans." A Currier & Ives lithograph by Louis Maurer is typical of many cartoons. It shows Fremont receiving the support of an overdressed black, a priest (a lie spread in the campaign was that Fremont was a Catholic), an elderly spinster in favor of free love, a ruffian worker holding a whisky bottle, a cigar-smoking feminist, and a puritanical reformer. A pro-Fillmore cartoon shows him in a carriage winning the presidential race, with Buchanan on Pierce's back in second place, and Fremont, in a cart, last, stuck in the "Abolition Cess Pool." Another pro-Fillmore cartoon, remarkable for its accurate portraiture, shows Fillmore as "The Right Man in the Right Place," in the middle between the gun-bearing Fremont with his sectional appeal to the North and the knife-slinging Buchanan with his appeal to the South.

Along with mudslinging against the candidates, the issue of slavery appeared with increasing frequency in cartoons. An elaborate cartoon called "The Slavery Monster" shows Buchanan mounted on a hideous dragonlike monster that is on a flatcar being pulled over the Mason-Dixon Line into Kansas by three doughfaces. In the distance, Fremont, on horseback, orders the monster back. Fillmore straddles the "fence" of the Mason-Dixon Line. Buchanan urges pulling down the fence and making room for the "Peculiar Institution," as Southerners referred to slavery. Another telling cartoon mocked

"The Slavery Monster" with Democratic candidate Buchanan on its back in 1856.

Southern claims as the controlling power of the world by depicting the South as a cotton ball held up by a slave, the real strength of the South. There is a grim humor in a cartoon about John Brown's raid on Harpers Ferry. Brown captured the armory and waited for nearby slaves to revolt and join him, but he was quickly captured and hanged. The cartoon shows Brown thrusting a spear at a slave: "Here! Take this and follow me!" The slave tells him: "Please God, Mr. Brown, dat is onpossible. We ain't done seedin' yit at our house."

A cartoon that appeared as Buchanan was leaving office dramatically illustrates the brewing national crisis. It is unusual, too, because no human figures are represented. At the left is the American eagle pictured when Buchanan took office: a symbol of strength, strong and defiant. At the right is the same national bird when Buchanan left office in 1861: broken and dejected, shorn of its proud feathers and sharp talons, standing on two wooden stumps labeled "Anarchy" and "Secession." As Buchanan's term ended, Southerners were withdrawing from Congress and the Confederacy had been declared. The election of 1860 would be the most fateful in American history, determining whether the nation would have peace or war.

CHAPTER X

In 1860, "Honest Abe" Lincoln, the rail splitter from Illinois, took the oath of office as President not of the United States of America but of the disunited states of America. His election had set in motion the last stages of the "irrepressible conflict." Seven Southern states had seceded and more were teetering. Behind Lincoln as he took the oath, were the girders of the unfinished dome of the Capitol, which seemed to symbolize the imperfect state of the union.

The disunity in the nation assured Lincoln of winning the election once he had overcome the formidable obstacles to his party's nomination. The Republicans had passed over their leading candidates to pick him, a man born in a log cabin, a farmer and fence-rail splitter, a country lawyer who had served one term in Congress and lost a Senate race in Illinois to Stephen A. Douglas. The Democrats had split wide open over slavery: Northern Democrats picked Senator Douglas; Southern Democrats put up a candidate of their own. With the Democrats divided, Lincoln carried the solid North and the election.

Southerners sneered at the "baboon" Lincoln, but the Republicans played up his lankiness, his homespun qualities. While conceding he was not handsome, Republicans dryly observed that if all the ugly men voted for him, he was a shoo-in. They made rail splitting the favorite cartoon theme of the campaign. The most economical cartoon was a head of Lincoln with a rail as a torso, two rails as arms and two more as legs, done by Frank Bellew, an English cartoonist newly arrived in the United States.

From the beginning, cartoonists rarely presented Lincoln as a statesman. One of the first cartoons of Lincoln shows him in a short-waisted swallowtail and thin pants, an outfit ill fitting his six-foot-four-inch frame. He was

A contemporary caricature of Abe Lincoln.

depicted as angular, with big feet and clothes too short for his long arms and legs. Another early representation comes from Cincinnati, often called "Porkopolis" in those days because of its meat-packing industry. A hog with the face of President Buchanan is being propelled toward a proslavery position by Senator Douglas; a shirt-sleeved Lincoln, with a butcher's apron and a club, is blocking the way. The cartoon is entitled "The Irrepressible Conflict," the term used by Senator William Seward of New York in a Senate speech to refer to the slavery issue: "an irrepressible conflict between opposing and enduring forces." (The hard-line speech may have cost him the nomination Lincoln won.) The cartoon was one of a number inspired by the famous Lincoln-Douglas debates in their 1858 Senate contest. In undertaking the contest, Lincoln sounded his theme: "A house divided against itself cannot stand. I believe this government cannot endure permanently half slave and half free." Another cartoon shows a smiling Lincoln telling a doleful Douglas that splitting fence rails is better politics than fencing with compromise positions on "Bleeding Kansas" and other slavery issues.

The debates were covered by the nation's newspapers, so that the two debaters had an unseen audience of millions as well as live audiences of thousands. Lincoln's "house divided" phrase gave rise to cartoons: one shows Lincoln dipping a brush in a pot called "Union Glue" to mend the crack between North and South.

The two protagonists, Douglas five feet and four inches of solid flesh, and Lincoln, tall and gawky, with deep-set eyes, appear all over again for the main event, the presidential election. There are the traditional sports con-

"A Job for the New Cabinet Maker," published in Frank Leslie's Illustrated Newspaper in 1861, portrayed Lincoln gluing the North and South together.

tests, a boxing match between the two with the White House awaiting the winner. There are the baseball players—Lincoln and the three other candidates—in a cartoon about the "national game." There is the race between the squat Douglas and the towering Lincoln to get over a rail fence in front of the White House. A black figure between the rails says to Douglas the unwelcome words of the slavery issue: "You find me in dis yer fence, Massa Duglis."

A daredevil stunt provided a new idea for cartoonists: Charles Blondin, a French acrobat, crossed Niagara Falls on a tightrope in 1859. One cartoon shows Lincoln in acrobat costume bearing a slave baby and a balancing pole. Another cartoon shows "Political Blondins" crossing the chasm between North and South. The lengthy balloons of comment suggest that the chasm cannot be spanned. Another shows Lincoln on a tightrope with a black on his shoulders and a balancing pole called "Constitution."

The attractions of the great showman, P. T. Barnum, also inspired cartoons. A strange creature whom Barnum called "What Is It?" appears as a black hailed by Lincoln as an "intellectual and noble creature" and future president. Siamese twins exhibited by Barnum become candidates about to be carved apart in the "Wonderful Surgical Operation Performed by Doct. Lincoln on the Political Chang and Eng." Another kind of feat is shown in "Honest Abe Taking Them on the Half Shell"; he is about to gulp down his divided soft-shell and hard-shell Democratic foes.

Rail splitting was the favorite cartoon theme for both those for and those against Lincoln. His supporters had

103

"Lincoln, Douglas, and the Rail-Fence Handicap"

organized Wide Awake Clubs and tramped the streets in military caps and capes carrying torches. Lincoln is shown in Wide Awake costume,. bearing a rail like a spear, breaking up an attempt by his rivals to break into the White House. "The Political Gymnasium" shows the candidates performing on equipment made of rails. All are tumbling or getting banged up except Lincoln, securely poised on his horizontal rail bar.

A widely circulated Currier & Ives lithograph (shown earlier) shows Lincoln being carried on a rail to the lunatic asylum by Horace Greeley, the great Northern newspaper editor and foe of slavery. The pair are followed by an array of crackpots. In another cartoon, Greeley and a black carry Lincoln on a rail labeled "Republican Platform." Greeley says Lincoln's rail splitting will ensure his election. The black says, "It's awful hard work carrying Old Massa Abe on nothing but dis ere rail." And Lincoln himself, in the Democratic cartoon, says: "It is true I have split rails but I begin to feel as if this rail would split me; it's the hardest stick I ever straddled."

Another cartoon, called "The Political Rail Splitter," shows Lincoln, with an ax whose head is that of a black, splitting the Union in two. Other cartoons show Lincoln riding a rail like a hobbyhorse and using a rail as a lever to dislodge the Democrats, and in many other ways. Another cartoon makes a wry comment to the effect that Lincoln became a minority president, outvoted by the combined opposition. It shows the other candidates over a kettle called "Union Broth" and points out, "Too Many Cooks Spoil the Broth." Incidentally, up to the time of his election, Lincoln was beardless. While still in Illinois,

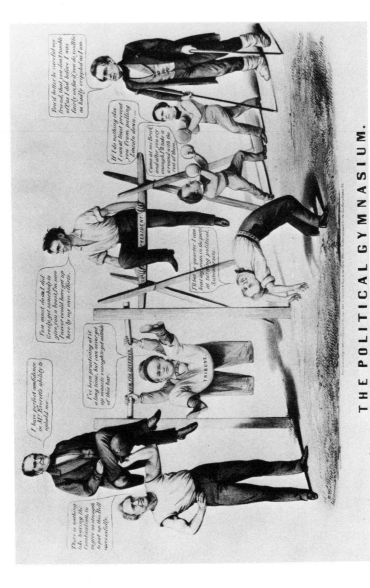

THE POLITICAL GYMNASIUM.

Lincoln straddles a rail fence in an 1860 Currier & Ives cartoon.

preparing to journey to Washington, he grew the first beard ever seen on a President. A cartoon quickly emerged called "Mr. Lincoln Sets a Style." It shows a plaster head of the bearded Lincoln under a sign, "Agency for the Lincoln Whiskeropherous." A druggist is telling a young man to try his concoctions "and in three weeks get a beard." A Northern view shows Lincoln as a schoolmaster at the Secession school taking action to round up his truant pupils. Thomas Nast, destined to become America's most noted cartoonist, pictured the Lincoln inauguration in what was probably his first political cartoon. It shows Lincoln as viewed by the North and the South. To the North he was a laureled goddess holding scales of justice and extending an olive branch of peace. To the South, he was an vicious armored god of war with a bloody sword, thunderbolts streaming from the eagle perched on his helmet.

At the time Lincoln took the oath, a Confederate government was functioning in the South, with Jefferson Davis as its head. A cartoon epitomizes Lincoln's immediate dilemma. It shows Lincoln in a circus's center ring, doing a "Great Feat of Balancing"—Peace or War. On a rod on his forehead he balances the dove of peace and Fort Sumter, the Union fort off Charleston, South Carolina. The balancing act had ended, and with it more than forty years of political compromises, with the first shots of the Civil War—Southern mortars firing on Fort Sumter.

The first years of the war went badly for the North, and Lincoln bore the brunt of the reproaches for the reverses on the battlefield and the ineptness of his generals. A Southern cartoon jibes at Lincoln's troubles with

A Thomas Nast cartoon depicting Lincoln as viewed by the North and South—as peacemaker and conqueror.

his generals, showing him as a schoolmaster trying to get results from four lamed and bandaged boys before him while others, wearing dunce caps, watch. Some of the fiercest anti-Lincoln cartoons came from England, where the Southern cause was viewed with much sympathy, largely out of material interest. England's foremost cartoonist, John Tenniel, who is famed also for his illustrations for *Alice in Wonderland,* took pains to depict an awkward, desperate man. His "Great Cannon Game" shows a billiard match where a sturdy, cocky Jefferson Davis disposes of one ball after another, while an ugly, sullen Lincoln says, "I wish I could make a few winning shots for a change."

An American cartoon shows a Union soldier presenting to Lincoln, who is a picture of dismay, a promissory note, a reminder that in Lincoln's first call for volunteers, he promised to subdue the South in ninety days. Behind Lincoln's back are the copperheads, a large fifth column of Southern sympathizers in the North. Their threat was expressed in a cartoon showing a feminine figure with drawn sword and shield, symbolizing the Union, at bay before writhing serpents with the faces of copperhead congressmen, all foes of the war.

In 1863, with victories at Gettysburg and Vicksburg, the tide turned in favor of the North. Lincoln made two master strokes. His Emancipation Proclamation granted freedom to slaves in the Confederate states. It was the most telling political stroke of the war: world opinion switched decisively to the North. The Gettysburg Address was a victory with words. Tennial put his own interpretation on the proclamation in a cartoon, "Abe Lincoln's Last Card." He showed a desperate President throwing down a card while his Southern opponent, holding the winning card, smiles in anticipation of victory. As usual, Tenniel shows Lincoln with legs sprawling, hair that looks like devil's horns, and a jutting jaw suggesting unpleasant toughness. In another brutal cartoon, "The Federal Phoenix," Tenniel depicts Lincoln as the bird of legend consumed by fire and rising from its ashes. A malevolent Lincoln, looking like a bird of prey, arises from the fire that consumes the Bill of Rights.

The national election of 1864 came in the midst of the Civil War. The high-running emotions in the bitterly fought election are reflected in two cartoons. In one, Columbia demands an accounting of killed Union soldiers as Lincoln cowers behind a general. But the other, by Thomas Nast, is against any appeasement of the South, contrasting an arrogant Jefferson Davis with a weeping Columbia by an open grave and a Union soldier with a leg missing. The cartoon was reproduced by the millions by the Republicans and helped bring about Lincoln's re-election.

Lincoln, despite heavy opposition in his own Republican party, was renominated. The Democrats' candidate was George B. McClellan, the top Union general for fifteen months before Lincoln fired him as a chronic staller and brought in General Ulysses S. Grant. The situation received fine graphic treatment in one of the best war cartoons. Grant is shown as a bulldog ready to fight to take Richmond. Down a way is a kennel, labeled "Richmond," occupied by a pack of cowardly yelping hounds. McClellan is telling the bulldog's master: "Uncle Abraham, don't you think you had better call the old dog off.

I'm afraid he'll hurt the other dogs." Lincoln answers: "Why, little Mac, that's the same pack of curs that chased you two years ago. They are pretty nearly used up now, and I think it's best to go in and finish them." Another cartoon shows "Little Mac, in His Great Two-Horse Act." He is shown as a circus rider trying in vain to ride the horses War and Peace. The Democrats hit the peace theme, expressed in a cartoon showing McClellan restraining Lincoln and Jefferson Davis from tearing the Union apart. Borrowing from Shakespeare, "Hamlet"-McClellan holds Lincoln's head, saying "I knew him, Horatio, a fellow of infinite jest." Another cartoon brands the whole Cabinet as dunces and incompetents, with Lincoln in the featured spot as a buffoon. An effective pro-Lincoln cartoon shows him as a confident giant holding the political pygmy McClellan in the palm of his hand. Little Mac holds a spade, a reference to a campaign charge that his army dug more than it fought.

Early in the campaign Lincoln told a story about a Dutch farmer whose advice was always, "It is not best to swap horses while crossing a stream." "Don't swap horses" became a neat campaign slogan, expressed in a cartoon that shows a horse with Lincoln's face being ridden by Brother Jonathan as the symbol of the United States. A horse with McClellan's face is far off. Brother Jonathan is explaining to John Bull, the symbol of England, why he is sticking to the horse he is riding. The nation agreed, and Lincoln won a second term decisively. "Long Abraham a Little Longer" was the title of a cartoon making Lincoln look twelve feet high as a result of his victory.

The Union armies pressed on to victory after victory. Jefferson Davis, disguised in women's clothes, was cap-

Lincoln is a confident gaint, McClellan is a political pygmy in this cartoon.

John Tenniel's "Britannia Sympathizes with Columbia."

tured. On April 5, 1865, General Robert E. Lee surrendered to Grant. On April 14 Lincoln was assassinated. Two cartoonists on either side of the Atlantic expressed the nation's grief. Thomas Nast's was "Columbia Grieving at Lincoln's Bier." In England, John Tenniel expressed his and his nation's sympathy with a drawing "Britannia sympathizes with Columbia." Included in the drawing is an unshackled slave, mourning.

CHAPTER XI

THOMAS Nast, the most powerful and influential cartoonist America has ever produced, came into his own in the decades after the Civil War, though Nast had already made his mark with his on-the-scene drawings of the battles between the North and South. As the bitterness of the war receded, the years saw the rise of great magazines of political satire and graphic humor and the emergence of an array of brilliant cartoonists, though they were overshadowed by Nast. The work of these cartoonists provides a tapestry of the aftermath of war, the arena of politics, and the growth of the United States into one of the great nations of the world by the end of the nineteenth century.

During his most productive years, Nast created or popularized a number of the most widely known and lasting symbols of American political life: the Republican elephant, the Democrat donkey, and the Tammany tiger, which became the symbol of the corrupt Democratic machine of New York City. He created the workingman's cap and dinner pail and the rag baby of currency infla-

A cartoon by Thomas Nast, creator of the Republican elephant.

tion. He was primarily responsible for the American image of Santa Claus, creating the jolly, roly-poly, bearded old gentleman from a Christmas-time character he remembered from his childhood in his native German village. The political symbols, first drawn in ridiculing and uncomplimentary fashion, have since been proudly and fondly adopted by the organizations they represent as part of their tradition. The Santa he created in 1866 became the one all boys and girls have remembered from that time forward.

In the great years of his career, when he was battling corrupt politicians in New York, he evolved a simple and forceful way of presenting a political cartoon. It became and has remained the pattern, the art form, of the American cartoons that followed. Even today, the variations are on Nast's basic style. In his work, Nast used a great deal of crosshatching, a shading device that keeps engravers from doing the carving routinely and allows the artist to express his style. In America, crosshatching seems to have become the distinguishing characteristic of the political cartoon. It converts a picture into a cartoon and gives it the look of a drawing done by a skilled cartoonist. Such is the influence of Thomas Nast that for years after photoengraving replaced wood engravers, cartoonists continued to use crosshatching. No wonder that Nast's younger contemporaries conferred on him during his lifetime the title, "father of the American political cartoon." Incidentally, along with establishing the simple style of modern American cartoons, Nast's captions were set in type under his drawings. In the days of wood engraving, it saved time: there was that much less wood to cut. To this day, the captions in American

"Merry Old Santa Claus" by Nast.

cartoons are still set in type, appearing either above or below the drawing.

Thomas Nast was born in 1840 in Germany and brought to the United States at the age of six. At sixteen, almost wholly self-taught, he became an artist for *Frank Leslie's Illustrated Newspaper*. He was twenty-four when, during the Civil War, President Lincoln said of him and his battlefield illustrations, "Thomas Nast has been our best recruiting sergeant." In 1862 Nast joined *Harper's Weekly*, and for the next quarter-century his name was joined with that of this illustrated weekly, the self-styled "Journal of Civilization." It was a good union. The magazine reflected his political views and gave him a perfect forum to express them. He brought to the magazine new heights of political cartooning and an immense following as the first great cartoonist to capture America's attention. The magazine became the greatest political power in publishing in the post–Civil War era.

As President Lincoln had pointed out earlier, Nast's cartoons had helped shape history, and they did so again after Lincoln's assassination. Nast was a good Republican all his life, but he was outraged by the Reconstruction policies of Lincoln's successor, President Andrew Johnson. Nast drew savage indictments of Johnson that showed him as a figure of weakness and malice, doing nothing as freed slaves were beaten and shot by bands of Southerners and old enemies of the Union returned to power. Nast's hero was President Ulysses S. Grant, and even his cartooning style changed when he drew Grant. Nast could tear into Horace Greeley, the great New York newspaper editor, when he ran against Grant for the presidency. But he ignored the scandalous laxity of the Grant administration and the fact that it was used by big business. Nast himself was never corrupt, rejecting fortunes offered to him.

Nast's fame and reputation as a crusader rest, above all, on some fifty cartoons he did in 1871 in his battle against corruption. In tandem with the *New York Times*, he took on—and brought down—the mighty "Boss" Tweed and his corrupt Tammany Ring, which was running New York City. Tammany was ready-made for Nast. It was Democrat, it was entrenched, and it broke the law flagrantly and constantly. Nast's bold, stark designs and elaborate crosshatching, which would have overpowered a lesser theme, were ideally suited for crimes of Tammany proportions. To take one instance: Tammany charged New York City almost $3 million for the work of one plasterer for nine months.

William M. Tweed looked at Thomas Nast's front-page cartoons in *Harper's Weekly* and all 300 pounds of him quivered with anger. He glared at the henchmen he had summoned to his office. "I t-tell you these pictures are d-dangerous and w-we g-gotta stop 'em," he declared. It was sometimes difficult to understand Tweed, who spoke with a sputtering volubility. But his point was clear. He didn't care what they wrote about him; his people couldn't read—*but they could see pictures.* His speech problem and enormous girth did not make him exactly the ideal candidate for public office. He could not stand to deliver a speech, nor could he sit in the chairs provided for public officials. When he served one term in the New York Senate, he kept getting stuck in the chairs.

But Tweed was supreme as a political boss, controlling New York through widespread election manipulation, extortion, contract padding, and pocket lining. He had gotten a running start as organizer and foreman of a volunteer fire company that had as its insignia the tiger that Tweed adopted as the symbol of his organization and Nast turned into the Tammany tiger. For the volunteer companies, putting out fires was often secondary to beating other companies to get there first. Tweed sometimes found beating up other companies a good way to beat them to fires. From this beginning he went into politics, starting with several minor offices; he was a drinking, licentious man with a faculty for making friends. He became leader of Tammany Hall, the Democratic organization of New York City, and he and his cohorts went to town. They controlled all city offices, even the lowest jobs, and the state legislature and took graft everywhere. In a period of twenty months, they wrung $200 million in graft out of New York City. Boss Tweed was the law, and the Tweed Ring was his creature.

Nast had begun sniping at the Tweed Ring but with little effect. Then in 1871 came proof of the gang's fraud and stealing. One of the Ring's members defected and turned over to the *New York Times* information from the city comptroller's ledgers. The way the Ring worked, financial statements were not made public. The *Times* editor was offered, and rejected, a million dollars for silence. The revelations came as the Ring was at the apex of its power, sure that no one could lay a glove on them. Then the *Times* started daily installments of the revelations, and Nast's weekly cartoons in *Harper's* translated them into devastating pictures.

The revelations gave Nast an opportunity to be in his glory, after waiting for a long time at the gates. He was now storming the castle, fighting for justice with the whole city finally becoming aroused. Nast opened fire with a cartoon in two parts, headed "Two Great Questions." An upper panel had Tweed and a bunch of cronies being asked what the Ingersoll Company was. It had just been revealed that the company had been paid $5 million. A lower panel asks, "Who Stole the People's Money?" Tweed and his followers are shown standing in a ring, each pointing an accusing finger at the one beside him and saying "It was him." This cartoon was what had set Tweed off on "stopping the pictures" because it was a one-two punch. It showed how the Ring operated, setting up phony companies, and it stirred up dissension about "taking the rap." Tweed wanted Nast stopped. At first, Nast received various kinds of threats, which he ignored.

The Ring resorted to new tactics. They determined to buy where they could not intimidate. An official of the bank the Ring used called on Nast to tell him some wealthy admirers believed study abroad would benefit him. They would put up $100,000 to underwrite it. Nast blinked. He was being asked not to draw cartoons for twenty times more than the $5,000 a year *Harper's* paid him to draw them. Nast blinked again and asked whether the banker thought his friends would put up $200,000. The banker pondered a bit, as bankers do when parting with money, then said: "From what I have heard at the bank they might. You have a great talent, but you need study, you need rest." Again Nast blinked. That kind of money would pay off the mortgage and make him comfortable for life. Then, quietly, almost talking to himself, Nast said he thought he could get his benefactors to go up to $500,000. "You can," said the banker scarcely hesitating.

Thomas Nast portrayed William Tweed as a vulture with its talons on the dead body of New York City in this cartoon.

No hemming and hawing this time; that was as high as he had been told to go. "You can," he said. "You can get five hundred thousand in gold to drop this Ring business and get out of the country."

Nast had played the game far enough, even though he savored being offered a fortune no other cartoonist had ever been or ever would be offered. "I don't think I'll do it," he told the banker. "I made up my mind to put those fellows behind bars and I'm going to do it."

Nast continued his cartoon attack with intense, dramatic, stark drawings, giving the leaders of the Ring a touch of grotesque fidelity that made them instantly recognizable. One shows the Ring's leaders as vultures on a mountain ledge surrounded by the bones of the city treasury, tax payers, law, and justice. The Tweed vulture has its talons on the dead body of New York City. Mountains are crumbling and lightning is striking all about them. It was a frequent Nast technique to caption his cartoons with statements by the men he was attacking. The Tammany mayor, the vulture with the eyeglasses, had said the fuss "will soon blow over." The cartoon's caption reads: "A Group of Vultures Waiting for the Storm to 'Blow Over'; Let Us Prey."

Another cartoon uses a visual pun as "The Only Way to Get Our Tammany Rulers on the Square." The square is a carpenter's square set up as a gallows with a noose at one end. Another Nast cartoon full of spirit and action shows the Tweed Ring in a mad race, pursuing each other, each shouting the accusing cry, "Stop Thief" to the next one.

Unsurpassed for sheer power was a cartoon of double-page size that was the climax of the campaign. The scene

125

is the coliseum in Rome. Seated in the box where the emperors sat, looking down with brutal, eager faces, are Tweed and his band. In the center of the amphitheater, with glaring eyes and gaping mouth, is a huge tiger, its great paws crushing down the fallen Republic, her symbolic sword broken, the helmet, labeled "ballot," smashed. In the distance are other fallen bodies. It was the first use of the Tammany tiger symbol, which was reinforced by the caption: "The Tammany Tiger Loose—What Are You Going to Do About It?" The *New York Times* called it "the most impressive political picture ever produced in this country." In the history of political cartoons it stands alone—today as then.

The Tweed Ring was voted out by the aroused voters. Again, Nast turned to the classical past for the essence of his triumph. Tweed, wounded, bandaged, disgusted, and disgusting, is shown as a general amid the ruins of Carthage, holding the hilt of a broken sword and a battered shield. The cartoon says "To the Victor Belong the Spoils."

As these cartoons suggest, Nast gave a new feeling for culture to Americans. In addition to his fondness for quotations from Shakespeare, he alluded to well-known paintings and often used them as models. He also quoted extensively from the statements of the men and newspapers he attacked, plastering their words on convenient spots in his cartoons to add to the force of his accusations. He also gave a new accuracy to the art of cartooning in America. His gift of twisting a face to make it both ridiculous and sinister without sacrificing recognizability was a departure from traditional cartooning.

During the campaign against the Tweed Ring, Nast

**A caricature of Tammany boss William Tweed by Thomas Nast,
"To the Victor Belongs the Spoils."**

William Tweed drawn by Thomas Nast.

created what may well be the perfect cartoon. It is a single figure, unusual for a Nast cartoon or others of the time. There are no words. It has the ingredients of humor, good drawing, a clear-cut message, and the unmistakable symbolism of money bags, which had not yet become a standard device. In addition to Tweed's immensity, the Boss is easily identified by his $15,000 diamond stickpin. The fulfilling touch is the head as a money bag, with a dollar sign suggesting a face.

CHAPTER XII

THE magazines of political cartoons and graphic humor that had begun in the 1830's and 1840's with, first, Philipon's *La Caricature* in Paris and then *Punch* in London, finally took root in the United States after the Civil War. The bitter divisions in the land and the war itself had preoccupied the nation. Even the two magazines that had come into existence shortly before the war, *Harper's Weekly* and *Frank Leslie's Illustrated Newspaper*, devoted themselves largely to depicting the clashes over slavery and the battle scenes of the conflict. When the war ended came more bitter issues: how to heal the wounds of war and reconcile North and South.

For the four decades until the end of the century, the country gave itself over to domestic growth and national expansion. It was a time when Americans moved into the last frontiers of the West, found gold, and established cattle kingdoms and the wheat farms of the homesteaders. It was a time for the growth of industry, of the railroad barons, of Andrew Carnegie, of John D. Rockefeller, of J. P. Morgan, of monopolies and trusts and a gospel of wealth. It was in this climate that magazines of political cartoons and satirical comment could flourish, finding everywhere shenanigans akin to those of Boss Tweed. The changing pattern of American life in a laissez-faire economy of burgeoning industry where "anything goes," provided new material for the cartoonists. Thomas Nast, the giant figure, overshadowed all others, but there were many man of talent turning their pens to the foibles, faults, and failures of a nation bound to fulfill its destiny, to become one of the great nations of the world.

The great influence on American cartoons was *Punch*, which over almost a century and a half has combined sophistication and joviality in a special blend that offered the choicest elements of British graphic art. *Punch* combined fun-poking graphic observations of social manners with political cartoons. The magazine was fortunate in having two great cartoonists on its staff. The first was John Leech, noted for his cartoons of the social scene, and the second was John Tenniel, who along with his prodigious output for *Punch*—more than 2,500 cartoons—did the exquisite illustrations for Lewis Carroll's *Alice in Wonderland* and *Through the Looking Glass*. Many of cartoonists' symbolic types are Tenniel creations: the Brother Jonathan version of Uncle Sam, the New Year, Columbia, Starvation, Disease, Death, Crime, Peace, War, Justice, Anarchy, the British Lion, the Russian bear, and the American eagle. Tenniel had a strong influence on the work of Nast.

As a matter of fact, it was an Englishman, a twenty-seven-year-old engraver named Henry Carter, who came to America in 1848 and brought into being the first successful publication of cartoons, articles, and illustrations. He started with a fashion monthly called *Frank Leslie's Ladies' Gazette of Fashion and Fancy Needlework,* which went well. He went on to found *Frank Leslie's Illustrated Newspaper,* a sixteen-page weekly with large, striking pictures and cartoons that usually followed the events they pictured by about two weeks—a speed in news illustration never before known in America. The events were of the sensational kind, like the fighting between proslavery and antislavery forces in Kansas, and it also featured sports, the arts, fashions, and serials.

To prepare big pictures in a hurry, the wood block for the engraving would be sawed into as many as thirty-two sections and each section given to a different engraver. More periodicals followed: *Frank Leslie's New Family Magazine, Frank Leslie's Budget of Fun,* and so on. The young Englishman legally changed his name to Frank Leslie. The magazine *Leslie's* led a crusade against the "swill milk" abuse. The dairies that supplied New York with milk were feeding their cows refuse from distilleries, with political protection. The foul dairies and the diseased, dying cows were relentlessly pictured in *Leslie's,* and in time the publication scored a complete victory. During the Civil War, the publication carried full-page folding battle scenes, which became a great pictorial history of the Civil War. *Leslie's* lasted until 1922.

A year after *Leslie's* came *Harper's Weekly,* which at first, as the product of book publishers, concentrated on serials by great English authors and on national and international commentary. But it swiftly turned to cartoons and pictures, though it avoided the sensationalism of *Leslie's.* It had the genius of Thomas Nast and other able cartoonists and artists, and provides a rich illustrated history from 1857 to 1916.

Even closer than any other American publication to the inimitable English *Punch* was *Puck,* founded as a humor magazine with cartoons in 1877. The founder was an artist from Vienna, Joseph Keppler, ably assisted by Barnard Gillam, another of the many talented English cartoonists. *Puck* attacked with humor and satire the political villains of the day, but it was the cartoons that provided the main fire power. Its keynote in its life of forty years was light humor. In 1881, *Puck* got a rival, *Judge,* founded by dissident artists who quit *Puck.* Again, two years later, in 1883, *Judge* got a rival called *Life,* which, less pungently, poked fun at the social customs, prejudices, and pretensions of the late-nineteenth-century middle class. This first *Life* was not the *Life* picture magazine of the 1930's but was, like its brethren, satiric in the words of its writers and the drawings of its artists. The cartoons and writing in these magazines made them perhaps the best humor magazines ever put out in America. Moreover, although dominated by the figures of Nast, Gillam, and Keppler, American graphic humor was rich in talent. Some of the three greats' important contemporaries were H. L. Stephens, Frank Bellew, Charles Dana Gibson, who created the Gibson Girl, and Frederick Burr Opper. Opper made his name at nineteen as a cartoonist for a magazine called *Wild Oats* and later became known for originating the strip cartoons. "Happy Holligan," "Maud the Donkey," and "Alphonse and Gaston" were comic creations by him beloved by several generations.

From the close of the Civil War until the 1890's, the

United States was turned inward, primarily concerned with its internal development. This was reflected in the cartoons, which in the aftermath of the war focused on the bitterness of the Reconstruction struggle and then went on to depict the sores, growing pains, and ailments—and power and muscle—of a nation developing its resources and moving to greatness. But first came the problem of reuniting the nation. President Andrew Johnson, essentially following Lincoln's policies, sought a reunion by peaceful means rather than by the sword. Many in Congress were opposed to his policies; they wanted a harsh peace. Johnson, an inept leader, encountered unyielding foes, who were especially angered when Johnson fired hard-line Cabinet members. Congress tried to impeach Johnson on trumped-up charges, but fell one vote short of success. H. L. Stephans in *Leslie's* depicted the struggle in eight small panels as "A Fight for the Championship," treating with comic spirit the grave question of whether Congress could strip a president of his powers and make him a President in name only. Nast spoke for Johnson's foes, depicting him as king executing those who had wanted the abolition of slavery, and celebrated Johnson's political death at the end of his term by borrowing from Shakespeare the scene when the conspirators kill Caesar and brandish their bloody daggers. The Romans all bear the faces of members of Congress.

Johnson was followed by Ulysses S. Grant, the most popular hero to emerge from the Civil War, who served for eight years. As a rule, generals do not make good presidents, and Grant was perhaps the most conspicuous example of the rule. He and his wife liked the expensive

THE POLITICAL DEATH OF THE BOGUS CÆSAR.

Nast's cartoon entitled, "The Political Death of the Bogus Caesar" was his comment on the 1868 impeachment of Andrew Johnson.

presents showered on them by men who did business with the government. Grant saw nothing wrong in that. He looked on rich men with a respect amounting to awe. He put a war profiteer in his Cabinet and made friends with the most celebrated thieves of Wall Street. He let his old army friends steal millions from the government simply because he could not believe anyone he liked was dishonest. Graft and corruption brought the morale of the government to an all-time low. The bad repute of the Grant years was worsened by a half dozen sickening scandals and a paralyzing financial panic. The whole atmosphere was wrapped up in a cartoon for *Leslie's* by Matt Morgan, an Englishman hired as a rival to Nast. In this particular cartoon, he matched Nast in savagery. He based it on the story of Belshazzar, the last king of Babylon, who, during a riotous feast, saw handwriting on the wall that was interpreted as a sign of doom. Morgan called his cartoon "Our Modern Belshazzar." It shows Grant sprawled on a throne, drunk, embracing a corrupt crony. He is surrounded by gifts, while grafting is being planned nearby. The words on the wall signify a growing sentiment for reform. A skilled draftsman, Morgan gives all his figures a compelling vividness. Morgan also showed Grant as a Roman emperor sitting on money bags while denying the pleas of needy veterans, and as a lecturer telling Boss Tweed that Tweed, unlike Grant, did not pocket enough to buy up everybody and thus make sure they would want him to keep running for office. Nast, to whom Grant was a hero, defended him, picturing him as a lion and his foes as mice.

Grant's successor, Rutherford B. Hayes, was the only President to take office with a cloud on his victory. He won by a single vote in the electoral college—185 to 184—as a result of Republican vote fraud in three Southern carpetbag states where federal troops were still stationed. The cheated Democrats were aroused almost to the point of starting another civil war. With Hayes, the era of Reconstruction in the South came to an end. The Republican and Democratic leaders made a bargin. If the Democrats accepted Hayes as President, he would put an end to Reconstruction. In *Puck*, which supported Grant's Southern policy, James A. Wales depicted it by showing carpetbag governments supported by bayonets, while Hayes plows under the bloody shirt, symbol of sectional strife, and sews a new era. To a large degree this new era meant a return to white supremacy.

In addition, Hayes gave the country an honest administration and an improved civil service. But his changes and reforms left him without a party, as epitomized in a cartoon in *Puck* by Joseph Keppler. The cartoon depicts Hayes as Cinderella in a corner by the fire, with his qualities of "prosperity soup" and "hard work marmalade" on the stone and shelf around him. He is scorned by the haughty sisters, Grant and political leader Roscoe Conkling. Hayes was stuck between sides: not bold enough for the reformers, too independent for the regulars.

During Hayes's term the nation celebrated its hundredth birthday, Alexander Graham Bell had just invented the telephone, the Sioux Indians killed 212 U.S. cavalrymen in Custer's last stand, women were demanding the vote and Victoria Woodhull ran for President, and labor entered the picture. A railroad strike brought clashes between strikers and troops that cost fifty-seven lives in pitched battles. And labor began to appear in cartoons. A Keppler cartoon in *Puck* advocated the exclusion of cheap Chinese laborers who were depriving Americans of jobs. In the same period, Keppler drew a series of warm cartoons welcoming immigrants. One shows the American Ark of Refuge and Uncle Sam, arms outstretched, welcoming couples from oppressive regimes abroad—a cartoon also valid for these days. In a humorous cartoon, "Looking Backward," he depicts descendants of earlier immigrants, now Americanized, holding off aliens whose garb reminds them of their past.

As Nast faded, Keppler became one of his foremost successors. He took inspiration for many of his cartoons from the theater—he had once served as a stage designer. He favored colorful tableaux and was the first artist to apply color lithography to his cartoons; he was forever tinkering with color combinations. Whenever possible he liked to insert a landscape into his cartoons to show off his artistic talents. This gave many of his works a sense of space rare in cartoons, but was the despair of *Puck*'s business manager because of the cost. Unlike Nast, Keppler developed disciples who became a school of cartoonists.

Hayes, no forceful President, was through after one term. Some Republicans wanted to bring Grant back for a third term, but this was too much for most of them, and their choice was Senator James Garfield. Garfield, the last of the log-cabin candidates, was elected but several months later was assassinated. Garfield's opponent was another Civil War general, Winfield S. Hancock, "Hancock the Superb." The race was marked by the absence of political issues, so the behavior and private lives of the candidates became issues. A cartoon containing characteristic subject matter was one by Keppler called "Forbidding the Banns," suggesting that Garfield, who appears as the bride of Uncle Sam, was involved in a financial scandal (he was supposed to have taken $300), and the marriage must be halted because there is a little baby, the $300. Garfield says bashfully, "It was such a little one." Scandal was an oft-aired charge, but putting Garfield in the role of an unwed mother was audacious even for those less sensitive days and certain to evoke ribald chuckles. *Puck* pictured the 250-pound Hancock as Samson defying the Republican enemy with the jawbone of a Democratic donkey.

Chester A. Arthur, who succeeded the slain Garfield, looked more like a President than any man since Washington. He disregarded the bosses who had given him the position, fought fraud, opposed "pork-barrel" legislation, began building a new steel Navy, and, above all, set up a civil service merit system, as reflected in two laudatory cartoons. A Keppler cartoon, "A Presidential Conjurer," shows President Arthur doing card tricks to bring jobs under Civil Service jurisdiction. James A. Wales, the founder of *Judge,* shows "The Proper Thing": the President in the White House ignoring old cronies seeking favors and jobs. During the Arthur years, the railroads grew mighty, trusts and monopolies flourished and squeezed the economy, labor fought abuses and unions grew, farmers began to organize, the frontier disappeared, and the cities began to bulge. In this period, William H. Vanderbilt, the railroad magnate and the richest man in the world, said to a reporter in an unplanned burst of frankness: "The public be damned."

They were words that would help elect a Democrat, Grover Cleveland, as the next President.

President Arthur's reward for virtue was to be denied renomination by angered Republicans of all factions. Instead, they nominated James G. Blaine, a founder of the Republican party and a longtime political leader, who had also used public position to make a private fortune and served powerful special interests. The Democrats nominated Grover Cleveland, the reform governor of New York. The campaign reached the apex of personal abuse and mudslinging in American political cartoons. The tone was set by what a contemporary senator called "the most merciless and fatal representation of a public man." A cartoon in *Puck* by Bernard Gillam showed Blaine as "The Tattooed Man." It was a takeoff on a French painting that was in turn inspired by a Greek tale of how a Greek prostitute was freed when her defender exposed her beauty to the court. Blaine stands blushing, hiding his face, but on his body are tattooed all his dishonest actions. One observer of the period wrote that it made him "feel a certain irresistible thrill of loathing." To offset this, the Republicans dug into Cleveland's past and came up with their own bombshell: Cleveland had had an affair and acknowledged an illegitimate child. A Frank Beard cartoon pulled out all the stops. Called "Another Voice for Cleveland," it shows Cleveland tormented by the bawling illegitimate offspring in the mother's arms. The baby is crying "I want my Pa." Cleveland characteristically did not deny the basic facts and diminished the political damage.

More damaging to Blaine was a fund-raising dinner in New York, that he attended just before the election. A

This cartoon by Frank Beard entitled, "Another Voice for Cleveland," refers to an illegitimate child he acknowledged.

cartoon called "The Royal Feast of Belshazzar Blaine," showing him flanked by the "Money Kings," Vanderbilt, Carnegie, and Astor; it appeared in the *New York World*. Cartoonists liked drawing feasts. They provided something to chew on. Blaine lost the state of New York and with it the election, and after twenty-five years, the Democrats had the presidency again. Cleveland, who took the position that "public office is a public trust," got into trouble with Civil War veterans and big business. He lost when he ran for a second term, defeated by Benjamin Harrison, who was the great-grandson of a signer of the Declaration of Independence and grandson of a president, but himself a small man in a big job. Keppler liked to draw a tiny man almost covered by Grandpa's stovepipe hat and finally showed Uncle Sam searching for Harrison inside the hat. Keppler also drew "The National Grab Bag," showing Harrison and Congress giving billions to special interests. The essence of the times was captured by Keppler's "The Bosses of the Senate." The Senate is being filled with the richest men in the land. The cartoon shows them sitting in the chamber, and in the back of the chamber are corpulent figures representing the trusts they served—oil, copper, steel, insurance, rails, and utilities. The country, beset by strikes and farm troubles and fed up with excesses, turned to Grover Cleveland again in 1893. He became the only President ever reelected after defeat.

From the end of the Civil War to the end of the nineteenth century, the country was growing great, but it was not a time of greatness. In such times cartoonists thrived. As James L. Ford said of *Puck* (and it applied to all the other cartoon publications and cartoonists), they "shot folly as it flew, punctured shams and dealt with politics and other matters of serious import fearlessly, seriously, and, on the whole, truthfully." The cartoonists of the period were powers in the land.

The three last decades of the nineteenth century were a golden age for political cartoons. The Uncle Sam figure so familiar today emerged in his final form in this period, though, of course, there had been Uncle Sam figures as early as the War of 1812. It was Joseph Keppler who fastened the chin whiskers on Uncle Sam. In the years from 1870 to 1900, the work of the cartoonist was more widely discussed, more graphically drawn, fearlessly published, more influential than ever before.

CHAPTER XIII

A CARTOON by Victor Gillam in *Judge* exuberantly depicts the industrial giant that the United States had become by the turn of the century. It shows Uncle Sam sitting atop the United States in a worker's apron giving final shape to a locomotive. At his feet everywhere are machines and the products they produce. From across the Atlantic and Pacific many little figures thrust bags of money at Uncle Sam. American goods were being marketed all over the globe: International Harvester reapers, Singer sewing machines, typewriters, fountain pens, oil, steel, rails were familiar everywhere from China to Peru. The United States had become the workshop of the world, producing in 1900 nearly $20 billion worth of agricultural and manufactured goods.

The prosperity that the nation enjoyed under President William McKinley was reflected in cartoons by Victor Gillam and Grant Hamilton in *Judge*. The former shows Democrat William Jennings Bryan tilting at a windmill shaped like a dinner pail; the latter shows endless dinner pails reflecting prosperity. McKinley credited a good part of his election victories to the symbol of the full dinner pail. It was not all roses from the cartoonists, however. Frederick Opper, who had left *Puck* for a New York newspaper, was unequaled for sugar-coated barbs and a sting disguised with an aura of drollery. The trusts, in the persons of Carnegie, Rockefeller, Morgan, and Mellon held power in the country. Opper, in a series called "Alice in Plunderland," showed McKinley as the trusts' little boy. Vice-president Theodore Roosevelt, who was a Rough Rider in the Spanish-American War, is depicted riding a hobbyhorse.

The Spanish-American War, to a large degree a result of American cartoons' and news stories' whipping up the nation's war fever, represented for the United States a sharp break with its past: the nation was now a world power. The war really had two separate parts. It took ten weeks of fighting in Cuba, which was seeking freedom from Spain, to crush the Spanish navy and land forces. It took three years to crush 7 million Filipinos, who also had risen up against Spanish rule and wanted freedom, not American rule in exchange.

From the close of the Civil War to the closing years of the century, the United States was primarily concerned with its own development. It did not want to be involved in foreign entanglements, ("we'll keep out"), and it had laid down the Monroe Doctrine warning other powers to stay away from the Americas ("you keep out"). Once the continental boundaries had been reached and industrialization established, the United States began to look outward. America was bursting with a sense of power grounded in a vast increase in population, wealth, and the products of industry. "Expand or explode" was the keynote. So the United States went to war to free the Cubans after the sinking of the battleship *Maine* in Havana harbor. President William McKinley reluctantly bowed to the will of the people, who were on fire for war, having been heavily influenced by the rivalry between two great newspaper chains, one owned by Joseph Pulitzer and the other by William Randolph Hearst. In their battle for readers, they played on the feelings of the people with savage cartoons and fake atrocity pictures. In fact, one cartoonist even showed McKinley trying to hush the yellow press to keep their bellicosity from disturbing the golden goose of prosperity.

Most cartoonists followed the Hearst-Pulitzer lead in promoting war. One of the most vicious cartoons was done by Grant Hamilton for the cover of *Judge* after the sinking of the *Maine*. It shows Spain as a brutish savage with bloodied knife leaning over a tombstone marked "Maine." After the sinking of the *Maine*, Hearst's *Morning Journal* sold a million copies a day and Pulitzer's *World* sold 5 million papers a week.

The turn of the century marked the ascendancy of the newspaper cartoon and the decline of the colored political cartoons of the magazines. The great breakthrough for the newspaper cartoons had come with the cartoon already mentioned, Walt McDougall's "The Royal Feast of Belshazzar Blaine," which had swung the election to Cleveland. The magazine cartoons lost their punch for two reasons. They were so powerful that they made enemies. Republicans shunned *Puck* and Democrats boycotted *Judge,* making advertisers unhappy. In addition, Hearst and Pulitzer lured away many of the ablest cartoonists, though often not for cartoons but to draw colored comic strips for the Sunday "funny papers." Moreover, the newspapers demanded daily cartoons, instead of the leisurely one per week. The treatment was different, the time was short, and many magazine cartoonists could not make the transition.

A new breed of cartoonists came into being, as newspapers all over the country had need of political cartoons. With new cartoonists came new techniques, because the elaborate, crowded compositions of the past, in *Harper's, Leslie's, Puck,* and *Judge* were outdated. New newspaper cartoonists turned to a heavier use of symbols, to the quick summing up of a political situation. They used and standardized such symbols as the Republican elephant and the Democratic donkey. The daily newspaper cartoon was not so much a new language as it was a new method of expression. It was graphic shorthand; it was a deft, simple statement, drawn with economy of line and emphatic in its effect. Along with the growth of the newspaper cartoon came the four-color presses that made colored comics possible and made them big money makers. *Puck* and *Judge* not only lost readers but their ablest and most popular artists, artists whose work, through syndicates, came before the eyes of over a hundred million every day.

When President McKinley was assassinated in 1901, he was succeeded by Theodore Roosevelt, who at forty-three became the youngest President in history. He took office at a time when the United States, as a result of the Spanish-American War, had become a colonial power, having established firm control of the Caribbean and obtained possessions in the western Pacific. Roosevelt realized the dream of every American boy of his time;

he fought in a war, he shot lions, he became President. He was incurably boyish and bellicose and virile; he loved a fight. He took office promising to follow McKinley policies; the pledge lasted three months. Regarding foreign affairs, he adopted as his pet watchword: "Speak softly and carry a big stick, you will go far." With a big stick the United States could make its weight felt among nations without shouting; without it, shouting would do no good. He had both a big stick and a big voice. He instigated a revolution in Panama that set up a government that allowed the United States to build the Panama Canal. At home, he introduced measures to break up the trusts and to regulate business and industry more effectively, to give labor a "Square Deal," to curb monopoly, to prevent through conservation the ravaging of America's natural resources by predatory corporations. With Roosevelt began the Progressive Era in American history, which marked an end to "anything goes." He was a man of high-voltage energy, who made the White House a pulpit from which he expounded his views. The first president to be photographed frequently in action, he loved to have his picture taken and delighted in cartoons of himself, no matter how they lampooned his features. (He himself was a frustrated cartoonist—sketches peppered his letters to his children.) Only one cartoon made him angry: it showed him mounting a "war horse" with the wrong foot in the stirrup.

Roosevelt's ventures beyond the nation's borders, deeply satisfying to most Americans, provided rich material for the cartoonists. Never one to head an unpopular cause, Roosevelt sensed that the times demanded new domestic policies. His new Progressive policies provided more rich

A cartoon of Theodore Roosevelt and his "Big Stick."

material for cartoons. In addition, his exuberant temperament, his incessant strenuous activity, his teeth, his moustache, his thick-lensed glasses were the stuff of cartoons. He was a master phrase maker: "My hat's in the ring," "big stick," "muckrakers," "I feel like a bull moose"— all provided cartoonists with a steady diet of new themes. Many of the leading cartoonists at the turn of the century found in Roosevelt inspiration for their best work. Roosevelt claimed the dentist was easier on his teeth than the cartoonists, but he collected every drawing of himself that he could. A toy was even named for him. In 1902 President Roosevelt refused to shoot a cub during a bear hunt in Mississippi. Clifford Berrymar of the *Washington Post* drew a "Teddy Bear" to depict the scene. Children are still playing with teddy bears.

Cartoonists delighted in drawing Roosevelt, whose features made even the inept artist look talented. He could be made into a toothy gargoyle on a tower of truth or a toothy block of wood, for his Square Deal. His big stick took many forms: he wades into the Caribbean carrying it and pulling the American Navy, to make U.S. power felt by the Latin Americans; he swings it to settle a French-German squabble; he swings it in a circle, knocking dead all the evil trusts.

Roosevelt lashed out against "malefactors of great wealth" to keep control of growing protest and radicalism. An anti-Roosevelt cartoon shows him as Nero in a Roman chariot swinging his big stick at different groups pulling the chariot. Another cartoon shows him swinging his big stick and dictatorially stepping on the Constitution. The whole episode of how Roosevelt acquired the Panama Canal—"I took the Isthmus and started the Ca-

"The Big Stick in the Caribbean Sea," displays the power that Roosevelt thought he had.

nal"—was depicted in a cartoon showing a giant Roosevelt, the American Navy at his feet, digging up a spadeful of Panama dirt and flinging it at the capital of Colombia, which was "sandbagged" and forced to give up control of Panama. Most Americans shared the view of Homer Davenport in the New York *Evening Mail* in his best-known cartoon. It shows Uncle Sam, with a hand on Roosevelt's shoulder, beaming as he says, "After all's said and done, he's good enough for me." Another drawing shows two cartoonists hugging each other with joy before an easel bearing a likeness of Roosevelt, the subject of more cartoons than anyone in the half century that saw cartoons become a feature of American journalism.

Entering his second term, Theodore Roosevelt promised that "under no circumstances" would he seek reelection, words he later wished he had bitten off. But he gritted his teeth and kept his promise. He handpicked his successor, William Howard Taft, his secretary of war, who at about 350 pounds was the weightiest man ever to be President. Bernard Partridge, in a cartoon in *Punch*, shows the Rough Rider Roosevelt taking the presidential hurdles while Taft, like a blimp, hangs on to his bootstraps. Taft lacked Roosevelt's showmanship and glamor and was more conservative. He failed to move the country and he turned Roosevelt sour. When the Republicans stuck with Taft for a second term, Roosevelt became a third-party candidate, the choice of the Progressive "Bull Moose" party. "I feel like a bull moose," Roosevelt said as he began his race, and thus put antlers on his Progressive party. He also provided another great symbol for the cartoonists. They showed Roosevelt riding a snorting bull moose like a steed, with the elephant and donkey taking to the hills to escape it.

The result of the Republican split was predictable: they lost the election. One cartoonist drew both the moose and elephant battered and knocked out. Another showed Roosevelt leaning on his moose looking at a mirage. A third showed Humpty-Dumpty with Roosevelt's face taking a great fall from the Bull Moose party wall. The victor was a Democrat, Woodrow Wilson, who took over the presidency with promises to reform the country. A cartoonist in *Puck* summed up the scene in simple mathematical terms: an elephant divided by a bull moose equals Wilson on a donkey tipping his hat in victory.

Woodrow Wilson was only the second Democratic President since 1861 when he was elected in 1912. Wilson was not only a born reformer but a deeply religious man and an idealist who radiated righteous indignation. His name for his administration was "New Freedom," and he fought against the "triple wall of privilege"—he lowered tariffs, reduced the power of bankers by establishing a Federal Reserve System, and attacked the monopolies of the trusts with a Federal Trade Commission. The cartoonists could not do much with Wilson, who looked like the professor he was and was standoffish and incapable of unbending in public. They didn't try. In two cartoons hailing his reforms, he looks like himself. One shows "Diogenes" halting his search for an honest man to hand his lantern to Wilson; the other shows Wilson reading the death sentence to a corpulent "Money Trust" in a cell.

Wilson was an archfoe of imperialism and war. Yet he

authorized more armed interventions in Latin America than any of his predecessors. When World War I broke out in Europe, he urged strict neutrality and was re-elected on the slogan "He kept us out of war." In fact, cartoonist Rollin Kirby went so far as to draw Wilson's Republican opponent, Charles Evans Hughes, as the front man for the German Kaiser.

When the Germans began unrestricted submarine warfare and a U-boat sank the British liner *Lusitania* with more than 100 Americans among the 1,200 who lost their lives, the days of American neutrality were numbered. Most American cartoonists were not neutral but were against Germany and the "Beast of Berlin." As in the Spanish-American War, the cartoonists stirred the feelings most Americans felt. Cartoons showed "The Return of the Goth," a reference to the destruction of the Roman Empire by barbarians, and German "beasts" ravaging Belgium or wiping their bloody hands on an American flag or using the pointed German helmet to cover and put out the candle of civilization. When the Germans intensified the submarine war against all shipping and sank U.S. vessels, they pushed America into the war.

In 1917, with the United States in the war, cartoons became patriotic messages and cartoonists little more than government cheerleaders. One powerful antiwar cartoon came from one of a group of leftist radical cartoonists. Robert Minor, in *The Masses*, drew "At Last a Perfect Soldier," showing a headless giant in a recruiting office, standing before an examiner clapping his hands with joy. This contrasted with one of the most powerful and most famous drawings in support of the war: James

Diogenes says to Woodrow Wilson: "Take my Lantern, you need it more than I do."

James Montgomery Flagg's famous enlistment poster of Uncle Sam.

Montgomery Flagg's enlistment poster showing Uncle Sam with a pointing finger saying "I Want You." For most cartoonists, the favorite sport was drawing the hanging of the Kaiser.

When Germany was defeated, Wilson became the first U.S. President to go to Europe to work for a peace treaty; he called for the creation of the League of Nations, to avert future wars. The European nations did not share Wilson's idealism. In a prophetic cartoon in 1919, Boardman Robinson almost forecast World War II as he showed a feeble, bony hand holding a pen over the Versailles Treaty, a mouse already nibbling at it, and in the murky background a bird of prey hovering expectantly. At home, Republican senators were convinced that the less truck the United States had with the squabbling European powers, the better off the country would be. A cartoon by John McCutcheon in the *Chicago Tribune* showed Uncle Sam appalled as he watched European powers sowing the continent with seeds of future wars. The Senate balked at joining the League of Nations. Wilson took his campaign for the League to the country but almost immediately he fell ill. Jay Darling, in the *Des Moines Register,* summed up the situation by showing the Republican elephant as the only animal that would not enter the Ark of Peace. The country wanted a "Return to normalcy" and elected Warren Harding as President.

In the wake of World War I came the eighteenth and nineteenth amendments to the Constitution, which brought great social change to the nation: the former established Prohibition by outlawing the sale or manufacture of alcoholic beverages; the latter finally gave women the right to vote. The freedom—some would say license—of the so-called Roaring Twenties was accelerated by Prohibition, which fostered bootleggers and gangsterism and, because the antiliquor measures were so widely flouted, bred a widespread disrespect for the law. Voting rights for women, a long-fought battle, came about partly in consequence of the numbers of women who had worked in war plants in World War I, the increasing number graduating from high school and college and going to work, and the revolt against the conventions of the past.

To the cartoonists, both issues were satire provoking and humor loaded. Rollin Kirby invented Mr. Dry, a bluenose, sour-faced, top-hatted figure labeled "Prohibition." A cartoon in the *New York World* showed a lanky Mr. Dry questioning an elfin, red-suited figure with a white beard and a sack over his shoulder: "Whatcha got in that bag?" In the *Cleveland Plain Dealer*, James Donahey pictured women in the role of Washington and his men crossing the Delaware, flying the banner, "Votes for Women"; John Knott of the *Dallas News* showed two Adams, one Democrat and one Republican, seeing a new beauty in Eve, each male claiming it was his rib that made her a voter.

Harding, like Grant, was unable to detect the evil in his associates. While the people, unconcerned, enjoyed their "normalcy," his administration was beset by graft and thievery. Most shocking was the Teapot Dome scandal, which involved tapping the naval oil reserves of Teapot Dome in Wyoming by private oilmen, with the connivance of Cabinet members. Cartoons of steaming teapots appeared frequently.

Harding died during his first term and was succeeded in 1923 by Calvin Coolidge, his vice-president. Coolidge, a stern-faced Vermonter, embodied the New England virtues of honesty, morality, and frugality. As Will Rogers said, he "didn't do anything, but that's what the people wanted done." "Silent Cal" came to be known for his brilliant flashes of silence. He took a nap every day, his feet on the presidential desk. "He slept more than any other President, whether by day or night," H. L. Mencken once wrote. "Nero fiddled but Coolidge only snored."

While Coolidge napped at the White House, the nation was in an orgy of speculation, gambling billions on the stock market. Coolidge called it "a natural expansion of business," not something for the government to worry about, for "the business of America is business." He was followed by Herbert Hoover after a campaign in which the Republicans promised "two cars in every garage" and "two chickens in every pot." Hoover, a fabulously successful engineer, wore painfully high starched collars and was shy and stiff. He had a belief in industry, thrift, and self-reliance. Jay Darling drew a cartoon showing him with a blueprint looking over a train called "Machinery of Government": "Fine Opportunity for a Modern Engineer." Six months after his inauguration, on October 24, 1929, came Black Thursday, the devastating crash of the stock market. It was the death of the boom that was never going to end, the end of normalcy, the beginning of the Depression, the longest and most devastating depression in American experience.

CHAPTER XIV

INSTEAD of two cars in every garage and two chickens in every pot, there were only two chickens in the garage, in a devastating cartoon by Rollin Kirby in the *New York World,* as he recalled Hoover's promises. Where there had been a driveway, there was overgrown grass. Kirby, who won three Pulitzer prizes, was one of the leading cartoonists of the period, along with Daniel Fitzpatrick. President Hoover kept making more promises: "Prosperity is just around the corner" and "The worst has passed." But the Depression nightmare deepened. In 1930 there were 3 million unemployed, in 1933 there were 15 million; 5,000 banks shut their doors; one out of every four farms was sold to pay for taxes.

In the *St. Louis Post-Dispatch* Fitzpatrick disposed of Hoover's well-intended but futile words. His cartoon shows two men, down and out and homeless, in one of the shantytowns that were called Hoovervilles. They are reading a newspaper headlined "Hoover Speech." Fitzpatrick's caption is "It seems there wasn't any Depression at all." The grimness of the Depression is depicted in

Daniel Fitzpatrick's cartoon "Direct Relief in Missouri" shows the daily sum that the state gave to a needy family.

two Fitzpatrick cartoons. One shows a woman sitting on a box, her head in her hands, bent in despair over a table. Two children are by her. Entering the wretched house is the husband, his face a skull with features created out of "45¢ a Day." This was the daily sum the state of Missouri gave a needy family. The same somber treatment is used in the other cartoon showing a gaunt, grim-faced man receiving a bowl of soup. The caption, "One Person out of Every Ten" reflects the number of persons getting relief. Kirby placed few figures in his pictures and used a pencil rather than a brush or pen to outline the figures, completing his stark, powerful compositions with crayon on grained paper. Fitzpatrick also used crayon on grained paper, exploiting it as a shading device instead of crosshatching. The technique was particularly effective for portraying massive symbols. His cartoons made dark, brooding, powerful statements. Mood was the dominant characteristic in the work of both artists.

In 1932 the people elected a new President, Franklin D. Roosevelt. At his inauguration in 1933 he told the nation, "The only thing we have to fear is fear itself." He called his administration the "New Deal" to help the "forgotten man." With a "brain trust" of academic experts around him, Roosevelt attacked the Depression on all fronts, instituting measure after measure in his first hundred days. Programs exploded over the American landscape in a string of alphabet firecrackers—new boards, bureaus, agencies, all called by their initials. Clarence Batchelor of the *New York News* caught the atmosphere of hope in a cartoon showing Roosevelt shaking hands with a worker holding a pickax and labeled

"The Forgotten Man." The caption has the worker saying "Yes, you remembered me."

Most cartoonists were hostile to the New Deal and worried about the billions Roosevelt was pouring into the economy to revive it. This reaction to his "pump priming" of the economy was represented by a leaky pump wasting millions, or by a buxom bathing beauty going over her head into an ocean of debt while holding the hand of a scrawny taxpayer who is shouting "Come back!" For Halloween, in 1936, Darling showed Roosevelt and his aides as pranksters stealing a privy labeled "Private Rights." It was a grim period, a period of great suffering and strong political passions, and the cartoons reflected the times.

Like his distant cousin, Theodore Roosevelt, "FDR" was a great subject for the cartoonists, pro and con. Roosevelt radiated confidence and assurance, and they tried to capture this attitude, his way of throwing back his head with cockiness. They quickly picked up his pince-nez glasses, the prominent chin, the broad, urbane smile, the ever-present cigarette holder tilted at a jaunty angle. Roosevelt was a handicapped person, but cartoonists, pro or con, never showed him as physically disabled. Matching the impression he gave to the people, they always pictured him as a man of vigor and health.

Like Teddy Roosevelt, FDR usually enjoyed the cartoons of himself. Before he ran for a third term, breaking a two-term tradition going back to Washington, he kept the country in suspense. One of his favorite cartoons, by Ross Lewis of the *Milwaukee Journal*, carries the caption, "The Sphinx Speaks, But Says Nothing." The

Sphinx has Roosevelt's pince-nez, his cigarette holder, and a knowing look. When the Republicans tried to make a campaign issue of his dog Fala during his fourth-term race, Tom Little drew another of Roosevelt's favorites. It shows his little dog chasing a great big elephant, the caption a quotation from Roosevelt to the effect that Fala was furious about the attack.

A favorite of the cartoonists went into eclipse in Roosevelt's first term. The "Noble Experiment" of Prohibition was repealed, and it did away with the mortician-like figure of Mr. Dry. Creator Rollin Kirby officially buried him with the words: "I was almost sorry to see him go. I was almost getting fond of the bum." But, like all the other invaluable symbols of the cartoonist's art, he didn't fade away. He remains the symbol of the blue-nose moralist, outraged by the evils he sees everywhere.

Amidst the unrelieved grimness of the Depression came cartoons in a lighter vein, yet fully reflecting an appreciation of how Roosevelt was reviving and transforming the country. These appeared in the *New Yorker*, a magazine that appeared in 1925, at a time when *Puck* and *Judge* and *Life* had all gone downhill. The *New Yorker*'s best years coincided with the Depression. A cartoon by Soglow illustrates the magazine's tone. Apple vendors selling apples for five cents were at every corner, and the cartoonist depicted four. But one of the four, attending a crate of apples with an "unemployed" sign on it, is a top-hatted, cravated aristocrat with cane. The final touch: his pants have a patch at the left knee. Peter Arno drew an aristocratic group on their way to the newsreel theaters popular at the time "to hiss Roosevelt." Eleanor Roosevelt was an observer for her disabled husband,

"The Sphinx Speaks, But Says Nothing" is the caption of this Ross Lewis cartoon about Roosevelt running for a third term.

talking to thousands of everyday folk. This inspired Alan Dunn to depict a sergeant addressing trainees: "And hereafter if there is anything you don't like, come to me—don't write to Mrs. Roosevelt." One of the all-time classics, by Robert Day, shows two miners deep in the bowels of a coal mine, and one is exclaiming: "For gosh sakes, here comes Mrs. Roosevelt."

In a cartoon showing a threadbare Uncle Sam cooking

165

a can of beans as he reads the news from the outside world, Rollin Kirby linked the grim life in the nation to the grim events beyond America's shores. Japan was conquering Asia, and Hitlerism was sweeping over Europe. The Nazi swastika cast an ever growing shadow. In 1939, in a "lightning war," Hitler invaded Poland after making a deal with Russia. This caused Britain and France, as Poland's allies, to declare war on Germany, and World War II began. Most Americans, while sympathetic to the European democracies and against the Nazis, felt World War I had been fought in vain and wanted overwhelmingly to stay out of war. This was vividly expressed in a Pulitzer Prize–winning cartoon by C. C. Batchelor of the *New York Daily News*. It showed war as a skeleton-faced prostitute inviting a young man with the words, "Come on in, I'll treat you right. I used to know your daddy."

In "The Only Way We Can Save Her" in the *Chicago Tribune*, Carey Orr pictured Democracy on her knees before Uncle Sam, pleading, "Stay out for my sake as well as your own." But from the Midwest, the traditional home of American isolationism, two cartoonists, Fitzpatrick and Vaughn Shoemaker of the *Chicago Daily News*, tried to drive home the significance of the enslavement and murder of millions and the futility of ever appeasing dictators. Shoemaker showed Hitler in a cab directing the skeleton-driver to the next country he was overrunning, or he showed Uncle Sam freezing and buried in a snowstorm of Nazism, saying, "Let me alone, it's so peaceful." Fitzpatrick made the swastika into a kneeling person: the bottom segments of the symbol are the legs, one part is hands behind the back in chains, and the other part is the bent head.

"Come on in, I'll treat you right, I used to know your daddy." This is a Pulitzer Prize-winning cartoon of C. C. Batchelor.

Fitzpatrick explained his approach:

How to portray the new movement in cartoon language? Perhaps this is a good example of the distilling process a cartoonist indulges in. The swastika, emblem of the movement, was modified to depict the real nature of Nazism. It is pure pictorial language and as simple as a drawing by an early caveman. Later, I transformed the swastika into a huge, tumbling engine of destruction that I used on a number of occasions.

He used it often, making the swastika into a giant steam shovel, gulping up one country after another.

Japan's sneak attack on Pearl Harbor plunged the United States into World War II. But the Japanese forgot that when one stabs a powerful opponent, one must stab to kill. A wounded but powerful American giant was determined to crush the Japanese in the Pacific. Fitzpatrick put it succinctly with a cartoon that showed a Japanese soldier pulling on the end of the tail of a creature whose body is invisible, deep in a cave. The caption read: "Wait till he learns what he's got hold of."

Pearl Harbor had been preceded six months earlier by another sneak attack, Hitler's invasion of Russia. Hitler and Stalin had made a deal to divide the world. But when the two master double crossers squabbled, Hitler resolved to knock off Russia and then snuff out Britain. After Hitler launched his devastating attack on Russia, Roosevelt and British Prime Minister Churchill had a strange bedfellow, Stalin. Hitler's attack on Russia was a disaster and inspired Fitzpatrick to draw on a famous painting of Napoleon retreating from Moscow on a horse

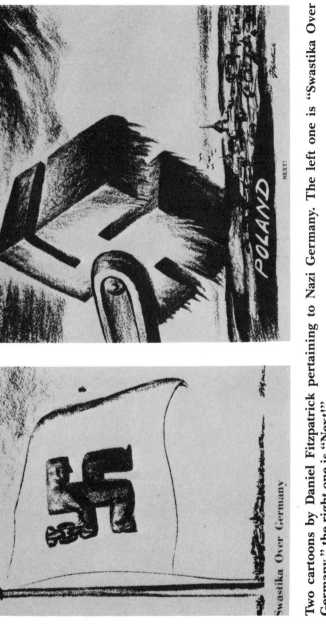

Two cartoons by Daniel Fitzpatrick pertaining to Nazi Germany. The left one is "Swastika Over Germany," the right one is "Next!"

struggling through the snow—only the face on the rider is Hitler's. Hitler was crushed by invading Allied armies and counterattacking Russians. Japan, going down to defeat with desperate resistance, surrendered when two atomic bombs were dropped on Hiroshima and Nagasaki. Victory came for the men in the foxholes, "Willie and Joe," unshaven and down to earth, as portrayed by Sergeant Bill Mauldin for an Army newspaper.

Victory came for the scientists who outraced the Germans in building the atomic bomb. But the bomb cast an ominous shadow over the postwar world. The bomb's significance, greater today than in 1945, was expressed by Jay Darling in a cartoon that shows the earth in fumes and charred chunks after an atomic war and a sole charred man using a battered pay telephone: "Hello, hello, if there is anyone left alive I'd like to unite with them in a world league to outlaw war." The hope that the victorious Allies would bring peace turned to dust, as predicted by a Manning cartoon in the Phoenix, Arizona, *Republican*. It showed Roosevelt, Churchill, and Stalin as the three musketeers. The Western leaders have their swords up in the classic "All for One, One for All" pose. Stalin has no sword; instead he clutches secret plans. There were hopes that the world would achieve peace through the Roosevelt-Churchill plan for a United Nations, far stronger than the old League of Nations. The hope was expressed in the simplest graphic terms by Fitzpatrick. It shows a mighty hand labeled "United Nations" grasping the hilt of a sword. It was captioned "United for war, why not for peace?"

The final defeat of Japan and the establishment of the United Nations came without President Roosevelt, who had died suddenly at the beginning of his fourth term in 1945. Roosevelt's oversized mantle had fallen on Vice-president Harry Truman. It was Truman who made the awesome decision to drop the bomb and who had to lead the nation in winning both the war and the peace. As the prophetic cartoon about the three musketeers had predicted, Russia and the West were soon at odds as Russia grabbed all of Eastern Europe and raised what Winston Churchill called the "Iron Curtain." The cartoonists had their symbol, the curtain, and used it, along with cartoons of Stalin clutching the globe, to illustrate the "cold war" between the Soviet bloc and the West.

The conflict between East and West carried over into the United Nations. This was illustrated by a cartoon by the great British cartoonist, David Low. It showed the United Nations Club, with Russia as a soccer player, Britain as a cricket player, the United States as a baseball player, and France as a tennis player. No one wanted to play anybody else's game, as he noted with his caption, "A fine team but it could do with a dash of unity."

President Truman was a prime mover in the establishment of the North Atlantic Treaty Organization to keep Russia from taking over all of Europe. Walt Kelly, better known as the creator of the political comic strip "Pogo," depicted the situation by showing Truman and Stalin in a "cold war" chess game. Stalin has plopped himself on the board and plunked his feet on Truman's lap to keep him from moving and force him to concede the game. But Truman is determined; his hands grasp the arms of the chair, conveying that he is ready to get up and fight. Truman's determination and steadfastness enabled him in 1948 to confound all the predictions and polls and, despite a divided Democratic party, gain a "miracle" up-set victory over Republican Thomas E. Dewey.

After the election, cartoonist Burt Talburt drew a fat man in a corner, who has written on his expansive back-side, "All us political experts." The caption was simply "Kick Me!"

The same gutsy quality was displayed in 1950, when the life of the infant UN hung in the balance. North Korea, in the Russian political sphere, invaded South Korea. President Truman met the challenge by ordering American forces, acting officially on behalf of the UN, to help defend South Korea. A cartoon by Low, called "History Doesn't Repeat Itself," shows Truman and a UN maiden rushing to the rescue, past the gravestone of the League of Nations, which had failed to act in similar circumstances. The Korean War was ultimately ended by a cease-fire after more than three years of fighting.

Harry Truman faced the gravest national and inter-national issues in a manner illustrated by a David Levine cartoon, which shows a man who is tough—he is wearing boxing gloves—yet who appears frank, open, and cheer-ful and radiates an expression that says, "Here I am doing the best I can."

In 1952, Dwight D. Eisenhower, the hero of the vic-tory over Germany in World War II, became President, and a young senator named Richard Nixon, who would go on to make his own unique place in American history, became vice-president.

CHAPTER XV

THE Eisenhower years were placid years, as the nation basked in the heroic "father image" it possessed in the man it had chosen as its leader. Ike's charm and simplicity inspired confidence, as did his broad grin, which the cartoonists played up. The cold war between the United States and Russia continued, put in a nutshell by *Punch* in a cartoon showing Eisenhower and Soviet leader Khrushchev arm wrestling. The growing fear of Communism was translated in the United States into a fear of anyone who held liberal views. This was exploited by Richard Nixon while he served in Congress and by Senator Joseph R. McCarthy, who made reckless and ill-founded accusations against countless people and gave his name to what became known as McCarthyism. McCarthy disregarded civil rights and even attacked Presidents Truman and Eisenhower. The atmosphere was depicted by Fitzpatrick, who showed vultures labeled "Hysteria" and "Spy Jitters" salivating over a corpse, labeled "Civil Liberties," hanging from a tree. The specific situation was pictured by a cartoon by Herbert Block,

"Handshake." A British view of Khrushchev and Eisenhower during the Cold War era.

who signed his cartoons "Herblock." It showed Eisenhower saying "Naughty, naughty" to McCarthy and Nixon, who were carrying buckets of paint for smearing. The cartoon was called "Rebuking the Mudslingers."

McCarthy finally went too far for the Senate, which censured him for conduct unbecoming a senator. With his many protest drawings, Block spearheaded the battle against the anti-Communist hysteria. He was the strongest crusading cartoonist since the days of Nast's attacks on Boss Tweed. Block's technique of heavy crayon shading was particularly effective in depicting McCarthy, who always looked unshaven and sinister. A typical Herblock cartoon picked up a favorite McCarthy expression, "I have here in my hand," and showed him holding "doctored photos" and "faked letters," all reeking. The Eisenhower years were marked by events that had significance beyond their immediate impact: the Supreme Court ruled that segregation of schools was unconstitutional, giving impetus to the civil rights movement, and the Russians sent up Sputnik I, the first space satellite, ushering in the space age.

There were other firsts when John F. Kennedy succeeded Eisenhower. He was the youngest man ever elected President and also the first Roman Catholic. For the first

Herblock's cartoon about Senator McCarthy with the caption: "I Have Here In My Hand—" —From *Herblock's Here And Now* (Simon & Schuster, 1955)

time, the world stood at the threshold of nuclear war. The Soviet Union attempted to establish nuclear weapons in Castro's Cuba, and these could have reached American shores. Kennedy demanded the Russians withdraw the weapons. Until the Russians did, the superpowers were poised for nuclear warfare and the whole world held its breath. The Cuban missile crisis was reduced to the simplest terms by Block in "Let's Get a Lock on This Thing." Kennedy and Khrushchev are pushing down the cover of a huge trunk labeled "Nuclear War," out of which a huge hand has already emerged. Several years into his presidency, Kennedy became, on a visit to Dallas, the fourth American President to be assassinated. The young President who, in his inaugural address, had told his fellow Americans, "Ask not what your country can do for you, ask what you can do for your country," had given his life for his country. Just about every cartoonist in the country sought to express the nation's grief, using recurrent themes: the Lincoln parallel, Kennedy's empty rocking chair, quotations from Kennedy, denunciation of violence and hate, the affirmation of continuity. Two of the most moving cartoons were a captionless cartoon by Mauldin of the statue of Lincoln in the Lincoln Memorial holding his face in his hands, and a Canadian cartoon of a saddened Statue of Liberty, the torch flameless, shedding a single tear. The same themes, with variations, emerged again after the attempted assassination of President Reagan in 1981.

The reins of office were taken over by Vice-president Lyndon B. Johnson, a Texan with the manner and speech of the Southwest frontier rather than the Northeast of the Kennedys. Long a leader of Congress, he knew how to "press the flesh," how to employ handshaking and cajoling techniques to persuade legislators. He brought into being the War on Poverty, to provide jobs, especially for youth, and oversaw passage of the Civil Rights Act, to enable blacks, who had been denied their voting rights in many areas, to exercise their civil rights. He named his administration and its programs the Great Society, an instrument to make Kennedy's dreams a reality. He was a man of colossal egotism and was determined to be ranked with Washington and Lincoln among the greatest presidents. Paul Szep, in the *Boston Globe,* struck at this hubris, depicting Johnson as an imperial ruler, his face expressing arrogance and false humility as he sits on a throne. A messenger is crawling up the steps with word that some senators are questioning Johnson's "infallibity."

On his way to creating the Great Society, President Johnson found instead an ugly war that consumed him— the war in Vietnam.

Under President Eisenhower, who sent financial aid, and Kennedy, who sent "advisors," the United States had become increasingly involved in Southeast Asia. President Johnson sent U.S. combat troops to South Vietnam to prevent a Communist takeover by North Vietnam. Pierre Bellocq, in the *Philadelphia Inquirer,* shows Johnson looking at an X-ray of black spots all over Vietnam and saying, "We've got to operate, and fast." Despite the infusion of more men and weapons, the war went badly. Mauldin showed one GI saying to another: "No, Hanson, you didn't find a box of bullets and two bags of rice. You captured an ammunition dump and a supply depot." A cartoon by David Levine in the *New York Review of Books* became a classic comment on rising opposition to the war. President Johnson had had an operation, and, with no inhibitions, bared his midriff to display his scar at a news conference. Levine's cartoon shows him doing just that, but the scar is in the shape of Vietnam. No words were needed. As the nation grew more divided about the war, Johnson announced he would not seek reelection. Szep showed what the step cost Johnson, drawing him about to commit hara-kiri, hunched over a sword labeled "Unity." But the cartoonist displayed compassion by showing Johnson's eyes closed and his mouth set, reflecting humility, acceptance, and determination.

"I am not a crook," said Lyndon Johnson's successor, Richard Nixon, the thirty-seventh President of the United States, in an attempt to reassure the American people of his integrity. Instead it was a indication of the low estate to which the presidency had sunk, perhaps the lowest in the history of the country. Nixon was the first President in history to resign his office, which he did in 1974, just a step or two ahead of impeachment proceedings. Virtually all of his top aides were sent to prison for a series of illegalities. The events were grouped under the heading "Watergate," because the débâcle began with an attempt by Nixon people to burglarize Democratic party headquarters in the Watergate Apartments in Washington.

Known as a "law and order" administration, President Nixon subverted the law to achieve the order he wanted. The Nixon administration wiretapped people illegally, illegally examined tax returns, primarily for the purpose of blackmail, and compiled an "enemies" list of opponents it feared. The President even had his own office

Lyndon B. Johnson in a caricature of him showing his scar in the shape of Vietnam. *Drawing by David Levine. Reprinted with permission from the New York Review of Books*© *1966. Nyrev Inc.*

tapped and taped. These tapes, especially ones so incriminating that they provided the "smoking gun" of guilt, led to his downfall.

All the elements of Watergate became grist for the cartoonists' mill as they portrayed the many facets of the situation. One prime target was President Nixon's claim of executive privilege, which he made to avoid giving up his tape recordings and having his aides testify. Tony Auth in the *Philadelphia Inquirer* drew a centipede a mile long with a Nixon face and the legs of aides rescued from testifying by the claim of executive privilege. Doug Marlette in the *Charlotte Observer* showed Nixon as the law-and-order "Superman" wearing a cloak of executive privilege that hides his henchmen. At his feet are burglar tools and tape recorders. Tony Auth showed Nixon and his secretary of state as two Atlases supporting the world, only Nixon's globe is a roll of tape. Paul Szep depicted the Nixon aides being removed from a paddy wagon with the caption "Snow White is still at large." Edmund Valtman, in the *Hartford Times,* shows Nixon pulling aside the window drapes to see a gallows, labeled "Impeachment," being tested. Paul Conrad of the *Los Angeles Times,* in an uncaptioned cartoon, pictured Nixon caught in the most intricate spiderweb ever spun. Not only was Nixon in Watergate trouble, he had escalated the Vietnam War by secretly invading Cambodia, an act that received little support and intensified opposition to the war. Paul Conrad, with characteristically bold strokes, pictured Nixon, shielded by the presidential seal, his hands fluttering in an unconvincing V-for-victory sign.

In *The New York Review of Books,* David Levine took Nast's cartoon of Tweed and his crew of vultures taking shelter from a storm and used it as a basis to portray the situation of the 1970's. He depicted the same scene, a cave in a mountain, with skeletons of past meals before the vultures. Like Tweed, Nixon is in the forefront, with a roll of tape around his neck. The two vultures behind

In a twofold strike, Herblock depicts Nixon desperately
bridging an unexplained gap in his incriminating tapes. He
voices the most remarkable words ever uttered by a president: "I am not a crook."—From *Herblock Special Report* (W.W.
Norton & Co., Inc., 1974)

him have the faces of his two closest aides. "It will soon blow over," Nast's caption for the lightning storm striking the mountain, was still apt, for Nixon too tried to "stonewall" Watergate as he tried to convince himself and others that the scandal was an insignificant episode.

None of the cartoonists was the equal of Herbert Block, a fact that Richard Nixon himself had recognized when he ran for the presidency against John F. Kennedy in 1960. Nixon is reported to have said in discussing his campaign strategy, "I have to erase the Herblock image." Block drew a cartoon that, as a friend of Nixon's said to Theodore H. White, "Nixon will never forget if he lives to be a hundred." It is captioned "Here he comes now" and shows a Republican welcoming committee rushing with surprise to greet Nixon—emerging from a sewer. Block, twice a Pulitzer Prize winner, ranks among the foremost contemporary cartoonists. He draws with an economy of style, without a wasted line, and his figures are instantly recognizable. His cartoons have been collected in numerous volumes, accompanied by an illuminating commentary by the artist, who also has a gift for expressing himself in words. More than any other cartoonist, he was to Richard Nixon what Thomas Nast was to Boss Tweed. He has influenced not only his times but his profession, for he has inspired a whole generation of followers. No one else could have created the uncaptioned cartoon of Nixon dangling in the wind, his hands clutching the ends of rolls of tape. One end of a tape says "I am . . ." and the other end says ". . . a Crook." In Nixon's mouth, as he gags on it, is the word "not."

Nixon left Washington and Gerald Ford took over. He was the first appointed—not elected—vice-president in

A caricature of Richard Nixon by Robert Pryor.

American history, named by Nixon following Vice-president Spiro Agnew's resignation because he was guilty of financial shenanigans. Nixon's resignation elevated Ford to the presidency. The Ford years were epitomized in a cartoon by Draper Hill in the *Commercial Appeal* of Memphis. It shows Ford trying to free himself from the coils of a serpent with a Nixon head and labeled with all the Watergate ills. Ford was accident-prone—he frequently bopped people in the head while golfing—and the cartoonists had a field day.

When Jimmy Carter became President, the cartoonists picked up his toothy smile to portray a President who otherwise lacked cartoon charisma. Picking up on the Paul Conrad cartoon of Nixon behind the seal of the President, Clyde Wells in the *Augusta Chronicle* depicted the American eagle on the President's seal with gleaming Carter teeth. Mike Peters in the *Dayton Daily News* drew the White House with teeth instead of columns at the entrance. Paul Conrad went so far as to symbolize Carter with just teeth, nothing else—like a set of upper and lower dentures. In another echo of the past, when the Carter budget director, Bert Lance, got investigated by Congress, Paul Szep had him saying what Nixon had said, and a little more: "I am not a crook . . . I'm a banker."

"Political cartoonists violate the rules of journalism, they often misquote, trifle with the truth, often make science fiction out of politics," says Jeff MacNelly of the *Richmond News Leader.* "But when the smoke clears, the political cartoonist has been getting closer to the truth than the guys who write political opinions." MacNelly is one of a new breed of young, brilliant cartoonists that have now come to the fore. In fact, there have never been so many good cartoonists—and rarely more wretched excesses and evils for their cartoons to dwell on. The decades since Thomas Nast have brought little change. Corruption is still with us, and so is the editorial cartoon, standing out amidst columns of black newsprint. In about sixteen square inches, this journalistic institution still manages to capture the essence of crises, expose pretensions, and cut down swollen egos—all with a few well-drawn strokes. A good cartoon is as powerful as a 1,000-watt spotlight; it provokes a gut reaction that not even the most stirring editorial can duplicate.

Cartoon onslaughts have their liabilities. The cartoon's first obligation is to be pithy: faces and facts may be stretched to make a point. Editorial cartoonists work best "against" rather than "for" something, the cartoon's tendency to present every issue in terms of black and white is not always appropriate. That lack of shading and subtlety influenced Adolph Ochs, the founder of the *New York Times,* to decide to use no cartoons on his paper's editorial page, a tradition that is still maintained today. "A cartoon," Ochs observed, cannot say " 'On the other hand.' " A cartoon can often do what prose cannot do: stimulate action by overstating—and sometimes overheating—an issue. The cartoon can provide a graphic perspective on these times or any other times. Nast's cartoon of the United States contending with inflation might have been drawn yesterday instead of a century ago. And the cartoon can provide a time capsule for the historian. William V. Shannon, *New York Times* editorial writer, predicted, perhaps wistfully, "A hundred years from now Herblock will be read and his cartoons admired by everyone trying to understand these strange times."

Nothing inspires familiar symbols and bromides like a deadline, and in the race against the clock, labels, clichés, and standard figures turn up often. But Bill Mauldin, a veteran of more than twenty years of editorial cartooning, says: "Cartoons are getting better, more and more away from labels. Readers are more savvy. It is less and less necessary to put names on things. The trend is more interesting drawing, less complicated captions." He adds, "A drawing with authority helps give authority to an idea, but there is no way a weak idea can make a good cartoon." Don Wright of the *Miami News* echoes the thought. "The editorial cartoon has become a welcome relief from some of the ponderous, overwritten poopery that typifies so many editorial pages today."

Changes are taking place in the American cartoon, which is striking out in new directions and exploring new forms. The giants of cartooning, Herblock, Paul Conrad, Bill Mauldin, and Patrick Oliphant, are being followed by a new group of cartoonists, men such as David Levine, Ranan Lurie, Robert Pryor, Edward Sorel, and Paul Szep. The cartoons are infused with subtler viewpoints and more pointed satire. Vietnam and Watergate shaped their indignation and forged their impartial impulse to bait the powerful. They attack from no fixed ideological position, turning their pens against Republicans or Democrats from one day to the next. They are also more fascinated with the absurdities of contemporary life than with preaching. The new art of political satire appears in the renewed popularity and sophistication of the comic strip. The initial impetus came from Jules Feiffer, who draws a strip cartoon for New York's *Village Voice* and *Playboy* and is also a playwright and film maker. The comic strip tradition has been carried much further by the immensely popular "Doonesbury," in which Garry Trudeau combines satire on politics and politicos with jibes at contemporary life, all with deftness and humor.

The cartoon has gained influence and clout in recent

years. Nothing damaged Johnson more than Levine's cartoon of LBJ lifting his shirt to reveal a gall-bladder scar in the shape of Vietnam. Richard Nixon is said to have observed that he wouldn't start the morning without looking at Herblock. The mood of the nation is skeptical. Historian Allan Nevins laid down the prerequisites for the cartoonist: "Wit and humor, truth, at least one side of the truth, and moral purpose."

As the United States moved into its third century as a nation, cartoonists have found a new realm to explore as they depict President Reagan's effort to turn back the clock to the days before Franklin D. Roosevelt and to the solid virtues of an America of simpler times. Only time will tell whether President Reagan can achieve what many regard as impossible. But a cartoonist can always do the impossible.

A cartoon by Jaf.

Index

188

189

About the Author

Samuel A. Tower began his newspaper career with the Associated Press in Washington, DC. He has since been with the *New York Times* as a Washington correspondent, a foreign editor, and more recently as director of educational and other special activities. He also writes the weekly column on stamp collecting in the Sunday *Times*. He has a B.A. from Yale University, magna cum laude, is a Phi Beta Kappa, and holds graduate degrees from Yale and Columbia.